These Are But Words

These Are But Words

An Anthology of Bomber Command Poems

Collected by Ken Marshall and Steve Allen

www.bombercommandbooks.com

BOMBER COMMAND BOOKS

An imprint of
MENTION THE WAR PUBLICATIONS

This edition first published 2020 by Mention the War Ltd., 25 Cromwell Street, Merthyr Tydfil, CF47 8RY.

Front cover painting "No Moon Tonight" by Simon W. Atack AGAVA.

www.simonatack.com.

Cover design: Topics - The Creative Partnership www.topicsdesign.co.uk

A CIP catalogue reference for this book is available from the British Library.

ISBN 9781911255611

Contents

Attribution of Poems

We have made a concerted effort to attribute each and every poem to its author and gained permission from them (or their next of kin - as most have now left us and gone to the big squadron reunion in the sky) prior to publishing. We sincerely apologise if we've been unsuccessful with tracing anyone along the line. We can assure you it was not for want of trying.

Many of the poems in this collection were written or submitted by members of the Air Gunners' Association, and originally published in their private newsletter, *The Turret*. The AGA was wound up in 2003 and it has not been possible to trace all those who contributed to it. All such poems are attributed to the original contributor as *Verse from The Turret*.

The poems are of considerable historical and literary interest and deserve to be shared to a wider audience. They also act as a permanent memorial to all those who served in Bomber Command, 1939-45.

We have given fully acknowledgement to the author, the relative, or the source of the poem wherever possible. If we have made an error, misquoted, or inadvertently misspelt the name of the author, we truly apologise. Any person disputing authorship of the poems or seeking their removal from future editions of this manuscript, is invited to contact our publisher, Mention the War Limited.

Our proceeds from the sales of this book will go to the upkeep and maintenance of the Bomber Command War Memorial, in Green Park. London. We do not seek to make any personal profit.

Per Ardua Ad Astra

Steve Allen and Ken Marshall. July 2020.

Introduction

Someone once said that there'd be no great poetry from the Second World War such as we had after the First. I like to think we've proved them wrong. Steve Allen and I first corresponded about 30 years ago, when I was researching my Dad's tour in Bomber Command for my book "The Pendulum and the Scythe". I discovered that Steve's Dad, Jim, was on 578 Squadron at the same time as my Dad and we've corresponded ever since, initially by post and then by e-mail as the technology evolved.

We started collecting Bomber Command poems when we both discovered that my father, and Steve's father in law, Arthur Pearce, who was a rear gunner in 156 PFF Squadron, had each been poets in their own right, and since then, like 'Topsy', the collection grew into this volume you now have in your hands. It's been a labour of love and respect for the brave boys (for that's all they were back then) of Bomber Command.

We both hope you enjoy reading it.

Ken Marshall.

1. Verse from The Turret

Bird Life - The Lesser Half-Brevet

Come all ye men of tongue and pen
Who spend your nights and days
By press of mike - just as you like
The pilot's deeds to praise
Publicity - it seems to me
Should still find time to sing
A song of love - in favour of –
The Bird of the Single Wing

Who mans the guns to keep the Huns
Off the back of the pilot's neck?
Who will twist and turn till his eyeballs burn
As he searches the sky for a speck?
Who will first expose his unfortunate nose
To the Focke Wulf's murderous sting?
Ask the pilot he'll tell you to see
The Bird of the Single Wing

And who must know all his radio
From 'A' to the bitter 'Z'?
Able to read what some clot has keyed
In a fit of insanity?
Who's got to crawl in a space so small
That a cat you could never swing?
This contortionist I present to you
Is the Bird of the Single Wing.

Who gets the girls with the heavenly curls
And the lips like a cupid's bow?
And sings out "Ooh, you Wonderful you,
How high do you really go?"
On whose manly chest does her little head rest,
As his nose gets set for the ring?
On the pilots of course - she'd have to use force
On the Bird of the Single Wing.

An Unknown New Zealand Air Gunner.

The Battle of Britain Memorial Flight

See that black magnificent war horse
As she leads the colts in play,
Three symbols of a mighty force
That kept our foes at bay,

Their teeth now drawn, they fract the sky,
Each Battle of Britain Day,
Such dauntless spirit cannot die
Or ever pass away.

It's sad to think they are on the brink of their life and soon must die,
But long may this historic link In the skies of Britain fly.

Frank Newton (35, 206, and 84 Squadrons).

Night Bombers

Eastwards they climb,
Black shapes against the grey
Of falling dusk.
Gone with the nodding day
From English fields.
Not theirs the sudden glow
Of triumph
That their fighter brothers know,
Only to fly through cloud,
Through storm, through night.
Unerring, and to keep
Their purpose bright,
Nor turn until
Their dreadful duty done,
Westward they climb
To race the awakened sun.

Anonymous.

Absent Friends

Still, I see them marching by
One by one,
Though I know their lives have gone
One by one
But they sing a happy song
And they call: "It won't be long-
Till you're marching – singing – with us."
One by one

And they tell us to be cheerful and be glad.
Sing and drink and laugh away,
Don't be sad.
Drink another for me
For very soon you'll be
Marching here with us – you'll see!
One by one

I see them in their flight
As off they go.
Dark in the fading light,
In sunset's glow.
And I hear the Merlin's roar,
As to the clouds they soar
Heading out towards the Ruhr,
One by one.

They were young – just boys – but men,
So long ago
Just how they all were then
We surely know
They would smile to hear us sing,
As we make the rafters ring;
Maybe they will all join in
One by one.

Anonymous.

Cologne 1942

The briefing room was crowded
With twenty crews, or more,
We saw the target map and route
And guessed what was in store.
The air is thick with rumour
"It's a Happy Valley treat,"
The C.O. enters quickly
We clatter to our feet.
"A message from the C-in-C"
We raise a muted groan,
"A thousand aircraft on tonight
Your target is Cologne."
"A thousand aircraft" echoes round,
A mocking cheer is raised,
"Four hundred Tiger Moths" one quips,
Yet still we are amazed.
"Your job tonight - to start the fires,
First there will find it tough,
Make it easy for the heavies
To drop their back-room stuff."
"A thousand aircraft on Cologne,
God help the bods below,
With a full moon and a clear sky
God help the sods that go."
The banter crackles back and forth,
Weak jokes that mask strong fears,
For some this night will end with death
With horror, grief and tears.
And so we saunter to the flights
Each with his thoughts alone,
Warsaw, Rotterdam, London burned,
For them – tonight Cologne.

George Cocker (218 Squadron)

It Will Never Happen to Me

"I'll always come back" said air-gunner Jack,
"That's one thing that I'll put my shirt on.
I feel quite safe sitting alone at the back,
It's not I who'll go for a burton"
But the Messerschmitt pilot had not heard this said
As he lined up his sights on the 'Lanc',
And Jack felt his parachute canopy spread,
As down into darkness he sank.

"They'll never get me" said the young WOP/AG,
To the rest of the boys in the flight.
"Twenty Ops - don't you see - Lady Luck flies with me,
She's with me by day and by night.
My Mickey-Mouse charm keeps me clear of all harm,
Friendly fortune takes care of our Bill"
But his luck went awry one night in the sky,
Through the shells of an eighty-eight mil.

"Of course I feel fear when the flak's very near,"
Said Sam who had guns at the front.
"When the moonshine is brighter, the heavens are lighter
And fighters are out on the hunt.
But my totem-pin wards me, my talisman guards me,
I trust and believe I'll come through"
But the flak came the wrong way and blew up the bomb-bay,
And Sam's gone to stay with his crew.

"I do not see why it just seems they all buy it"
Bert said to me up in the bar.
They're efficient and plucky - I guess we've been lucky,
We've each got a good guiding star.
We go off on ops, pull out all the stops,
Our good fortune ne'er seems to flag"
Now we're walking the wire - with less of our fire,
Together still - inside the bag!

Bill Rainford (38 Squadron).

Air Gunners' Day at Runnymede

Each year we climb the winding road;
The bowery, emerald treed;
The long road, the ancient road
That leads to Runnymede.

And there among the lettered walls
Where those who seek may trace,
We feel, within, a quiet pride
In this, our Island Race.

And those who came from lands afar
Who heard the Nation's cry,
In death are now our kith and kin;
Their names will never die.

No known graves have these, my friends,
No sacred, hallowed ground;
But we remember year by year,
When Spring time comes around.

And soon the Spring will come once more,
And we will meet again;
For their most true memorial
Is in the hearts of men.

So let us then remember these
Of our proud Nation's bred,
Whose names will live forever more
In stone at Runnymede.

Victor Cavendish (88, 106 and 83 Squadrons).

To My Wellington Bomber

When first we met I felt afraid,
      You looked so cumbersome and staid;
Standing quietly near some trees,
      Shuddering gently in the breeze,
It seemed incredible to me,
      That you and I would ever see
Vast tracts of German territory.

Do you remember our first flight?
      Climbing steadily through the night,
We went to Bremen, I believe-
      Or was it Kiel or Ludenschieve?
But anyhow I could surmise
      That in spite of your great size,
You loved your element, the skies.

Then the raid that we went through,
      Each one an epic, each one new;
Each one filled with thrills and fears,
      Sweating – sick – and near to tears;
Emden shot us up to hell,
      Hamburg, Gladbach, Köln as well.
Still, we came home, our tales to tell.

But, as before, on frenzied nights,
      You steeply dived – while curing lights
Of tracer shells ripped through your frame,
      Though cheating death brought us no fame.
And if one night we don't return,
      There will be another star to burn.
Brighter than the rest descending
      Reflecting on the clouds and lending
Glorious colours to our ending.

Anonymous, contributed by WOP/AG. G.E. Radford. (221 & 172 Squadrons).

A-Tapping His Finger a WOP/AG Sat

(With apologies to Gilbert and Sullivan)

At a key by a table a Wop/AG sat,
Going dit dit dah dit dit dah dit dit.
And I said to him "Wop/AG Why do you sit
Going dit dit dah dit dit dah dit dit."?
"I sit weakness of intellect", I cried
"Or a great NAAFI bun in your little inside"?
With a shake of his ruddy fathead he replied
"Oh dit dit dah dit dit dah dit dit".

"I was courting a lass who was lovely and fair,
Oh dit dit dah dit dit dah dit dit.
She had lovely blue eyes and languorous air,
Oh dit dit dah dit dit dah dit dit.
How I sighed o'er that maiden! I sighed and I sighed;
Oh please let me love you, my darling" I cried,
But she gave me a wallop that knocked me cross,-eyed,
Oh dit dit dah dit dit dah dit dit".

"The cold hearted maiden then left me of course,
Oh dit dit dah dit dit dah dit dit.
So I went the next day and joined the Air Force,
Oh dit dit dah dit dit dah dit dit.
At a square bashing centre I turned up one day
And I learnt all my drill and P.T. the hard way.
Every time I went wrong I could hear the Sarge say;
"You dit dit dah dit dit dah dit dit".

"To wireless and gunnery schools I then went
Learning dit dit dah dit dit dah dit dit.
And then to an ops Squadron I was next sent
Going dit dit dah dit dit dah dit dit.
On an ops trip one day I did dream of my lass
As I sat there day-dreaming it soon came to pass
That a dirty great shell travelled straight through
The glass – (well Perspdoesn't rhyme)
Of my dit dit dah dit dit dah dit dit".

This tale has a moral all you there below
With your dit dit dah dit dit dah dit dit.

The cause of my trouble as you will all know,
Was dit dit dah dit dit dah dit dit.
So when out on an Ops Trip sure you will agree,
On the lookout for trouble you always must be.
Or like me you'll spend all of eternity,
Going dit dit dah dit dit dah dit dit.

Victor Cavendish (88, 106 and 83 Squadrons).

Children of the Night

(Bomber Command 1939 – 1945)
The sun is slowly setting, and as it slips away,
A changing pattern of colour around one lies.
We feel so very humble as we watch the closing day,
And onward soars our plane across the skies.

This silent world of wonder means everything to me,
The storm and cloud, with wind and rainbow ring.
Round us there's a feeling, in our hearts that we
Are in the presence of the King of Kings.

The evening's velvet mantle gathers dark around us,
We feel like little children in the night,
As men the fear of darkness has not found us,
Still we seek comfort in the stars so bright.

As endless as the sky seems the long and weary night,
We laugh and talk though nerves are tightly drawn
And quietly we pray that he will guide our homeward flight,
And we will live to see the beauty of the dawn.

Jim Davis, ex-90 and 7 Squadrons

Air Gunner

The eye behind this gun made peace
With a boy's eye which doubted, trembled,
Guileless in the mocking light.
Of frontiers where death assembled.

Peace was as single as the dawn,
Flew straight as the birds migrating,
Timelessly in tune with time,
Purposeful, uncalculating.

So boyish doubt was put away;
The man's eye and the boy's were one.
Mockery and death retreat
Before the eye behind this gun,

John Pudney.

Security

Empty your pockets, Tom, Dick and Harry,
Strip your identity, leave it behind.
Lawyer, garage-hand, grocer, don't tarry
With your own country, with your own kind.

Leave all your letters, suburb and township,
Green fen and grocery, slip-away and bay,
Hot spring and prairie, smoke stack and coal tip,
Leave in our keeping while you're away.

Tom, Dick and Harry, plain names and numbers,
Pilot, Observer and Gunner depart.
Their personal litter only encumbers
Somebody's head, somebody's heart.

John Pudney

Night Flight

Lie in the dark and listen,
It's clear tonight so they're flying high,
Hundreds of them, thousands perhaps,
Riding the icy, moonlit sky,
Men, machinery, bombs and maps,
Altimeters and guns and charts,
Coffee, sandwiches, fleece-lined boots,
Bones and muscles and minds and hearts,
British saplings with British roots,
Deep in the earth they've left below,
Lie in the dark and let them go;
Lie in the dark and listen.

Lie in the dark and listen,
They're going over in waves and waves.
High above villages, hills and streams,
Country churches and little graves
And little citizens' worried dreams.
Very soon they'll have reached the sea,
And far below them will lie the bays
And cliffs and sands where they used to be
Taken for summer holidays.
Lie in the dark and let them go.
Theirs is a world you'll never know.
Lie in the dark and listen.

Lie in the dark and listen,
City magnates and steel contractors,
Factory workers and politicians,
Soft, hysterical little actors,
Ballet dancers, reserved musicians,
Safe in your warm civilian beds.
Count your profits and count your sheep;
Life is passing above your heads,
Just turn over and try to sleep.
Lie in the dark and let them go;
There's one debt you'll forever owe;
Lie in the dark and listen.

Attributed to Noel Coward, as published in Verse from The Turret.

23

Operation 'Mild and Bitter'

I wandered lonely as a 'Lanc'
Whose navigator's mind's a blank
When suddenly I saw the 'Red'
Which briefing officer had said
Should, somehow be upon my bow
And not ahead as it is now.

I eased to port across the stream
Of other 'bods' who, it would seem
Were more intent upon this course
And less upon the mighty force
Of one, whose load this dark night
Could be described as 'Dynamite'.

And so, despite some heavy 'jinking'
Which I'm reminded, rhymes with drinking,
I reached the turning point at last
Forgetting hazards which had passed;
And, thinking to impress my crew
Dived in the turn and followed through.

And now, the strangest part to tell,
I dived whilst singing 'William Tell'
The 'flak' or something missed the apple
But hit my head which seemed to rattle
Enough to send my addled senses
Into the realms of phantom frenzies.

But still the saddest bit of all
As on all fours I tried to crawl
A policeman, torch and buttons bright,
Assisted, sternly, to put me right,
While stating sternly in accents clear;
"You can't do that, sir – not right 'ere."

The moral to this flight of fancy
A lesson which I learnt so sadly
Never let the spirits guide you
After sinking pints inside you
If you must put 'red' on 'Red'
Don't use your nose and earthy bed.

To bomber types, this word of warning
The sky you used whilst subjects warring,
Was free of holes though not of lights
Or beacons, which were friendly sights.
But homing on the 'Penguin' version
Was not, I found, A 'light' diversion.

F.J. Kelsh

An Air Gunner's Lament

You helped 'em get their D.F.C.s
And, now and then odd O.B.E.s
Whilst down the back you sit and freeze
And just press on rewardless.

It seems to be a pilot's war,
They go on rest – you do four more;
But belt up son, you know the score,
You'll just press on rewardless.

It would be nice to win more rings
All up your sleeve – or gongs and things;
But till you wear a pilot's wings,
You'll just press on rewardless.

And when I reach St. Peter's door,
-It won't be long, I feel quite sure,
He'll ask; "Just what are you here for?
Shove off Jack" – Still rewardless.

Squadron Leader 'Dusty' Miller, ex-38, 69, 115, 148, 458 Squadrons.

A note was added to the text;- "Written, presumably, before 'Dusty's' rings started climbing up his arms!". One can only assume then, that 'Dusty' Miller was only a Flt/Sgt. when he wrote this and gained promotion later in his career.

Lest We Forget

One day a breed of men were born,
From every walk of life,
They came from near and far to fight,
For a certain way of life.

Some were tall and some were short,
And some were dark and lean,
And some spoke different languages,
But all were young and keen.

They all trained hard, and then one day,
A Wing Commander came
And pinned upon their breast, a badge,
Air Gunners they became.

A squadron was their final goal,
To join an aircraft crew,
On Wimpys, Lancs, and Stirlings,
And some Blenheims too.

They fought at night and in the day,
Their ops increased in number,
Some returned – and some did not,
For thirty was the number.

Some survived to reach this mark,
And some continued flying,
Some spent years behind the bars,
With many of them dying.

At last the victory came in sight,
The runways now are silent,
The echoes of the past remain,
A conflict, long, and violent.

This breed of men are now but few
But they remember others,
Who flew with them so long ago,
Their Royal Air Force brothers

Bunny Austin, ex-99 and 40 Squadrons

26

Sky Over Holland

When I look at the sky over Holland at night,
The blue dome and the stars are tranquil and bright.
It is peaceful and still, not a sound to be heard
But the rustling of leaves and the cry of a bird.

Not a bomber, no fighters on high any more,
And no criss-crossing searchlights as in days of war.
All is peaceful and still, for the Germans have gone,
For the battle for freedom was finally won.

When we sat in the path of the bombers at night,
We felt anxious but glad for, their every flight
Brought nearer the day when the Germans would flee,
When the war would be over, and we would be free.

We all prayed with great fervour and often cried out
"Oh Lord keep them safe, let them dive out
Of the crossroads of searchlights high up in the sky,
And please – save their lives God – Oh don't let them die"

The young children prayed: "Send us so many planes
That the sparrows can't fly and must walk in the lanes"
And the parents prayed: "Please, let them soon free us all
From the Teuton's mad fury that holds us in thrall."

Though so many were lost in the terrible fight,
While we prayed and watched anxiously many a night,
Their endeavours and courage have not been in vain,
For by them and their comrades, the Germans were slain.

When I looked at the sky over Holland last night,
The blue dome and the stars were all tranquil and bright.
There is peace, no more sirens, I hear a bird call;
Oh we thank you dear airmen – May God bless you all.

Maria Steinweg –Ten- Horn, Kerkweg, Heelsum, Holland

May 1979, in response to a visit made by Air Gunners to Arnhem.
Contributed by Air-Gunner K. Rendall. No 357 Squadron (S.E.A.F.)

Odd Ode to Air Gunners

Here is the tale of Gunner Joe,
Whose turret fluid refused to flow,
And though he was a brave young man,
He put his crew right in a jam.

I'll tell his story from the start
So those concerned may take to heart
The lesson that this odd ode teaches
And how he nearly lost his breeches.

One night when going hell for leather,
Flat out through really dirty weather,
Joe forgot what they had taught him
About the turret that he fought in.

Constant use to keep it hot –
Was just the part that Joe forgot
And so instead of quick reaction
Oil-drag made him lag a fraction.

Up above he saw a Hun
Diving down with blazing gun,
Trying hard to get a bead –
While Joe himself was short of speed.

Joe was shaken to the core
When he found his aim was poor.
"Coo" he said, his faith a-slipping,
"Are my oil pipes filled with dripping?"

Luckily the Hun went past
Falling to a comrade's blast,
Giving Joe some time to think
Of how he nearly hit the drink.

Here's his vow, made there and then –
"Take in all instructors' gen,
And practice hard as all advise,
When stooging in the upper skies.

Bill Hearn. (90 Squadron) (with apologies to Cyril Fletcher).

Are You Alright, Jack?

Are you alright Jack? I'm asking
For you're often on my mind.
As you journey on do you ever think
Of the pal you left behind?
I often think of you Jack
Do you ever think of me?
Do you still recall the good old times;
The days that used to be?

We met as little kids at school:
We hit it off at once,
Though you were such a bright lad,
And I was such a dunce.
Apart from my old widowed mum
I hadn't any kin,
And I loved you like a brother:
My pal through thick and thin.

We went through school together;
The glad days and the sad.
You shared with me the good times
And cheered me though the bad.
And then we went as 'prentices
On the local factory floor,
And I knew I took for granted
We'd be pals for evermore.

We finished our apprenticeships
With old Hitler coming strong,
So we upped and joined the R.A.F.
We went to "right the wrong"
We did our Morse together;
Our guns and O.T.U.
We joined the self-same squadron;
The very self-same crew.
I well recall those times
Though they're so long ago;
When you were our mid-upper
And I was tail end Joe.
Our tour was nearly at and end
We thought we'd won the race,

When another man went missing
And you'd to take his place.

Of course I went to see you go;
You grinned and winked your eye.
I never thought as you went off
We'd said our last goodbye.
I've grieved for you a long time,
The days seem bleak and drear,
And I know I still remember
Each day of every year.

It's been a lonely road since then
But I've conquered every hill.
There was a time I wouldn't fight
But you gave me the will.
You have "No known grave" Jack,
And little claim to fame.
But on that wall at Runnymede
I know they've carved your name.

I sometimes sit and ponder
For only God can tell;
But you always were a man Jack
And you made me one as well.
Are you alright Jack? I'm sure you are,
For you're often on my mind,
And I know you're up there waiting
For the pal you left behind.

Victor Cavendish (88, 106 and 83 Squadrons)

Of all the poems I've had to read and type, this has been the hardest and most moving – SCA.

Memories

Oft did I see a second sunset glow,
As high we climbed the dusk-filled sky,
Dark fields below,
Higher yet, unto a faery scene,
Cloud tops gleaming
White and clean,
So beautiful they seemed unreal,
A vision from a lovely dream.
>But helmed and masked, a faceless pawn,
>I have seen great cities burn,
>As with a bright red ruby glare
>Our markers hang upon the air
>To say "Press on…for this is where
>Death and destruction shall declare,
>The Sack of Troy was but child's play
>Against what man can do today".
And may times like falling stars
Other planes and other pawns
Have plunged to earth as I did stare
And count the reaper's tale of we
Who were his quarry through his friends.
>Yet through it all, so constantly,
>A kind of beauty did I see,
>In moonlight's gleam…in searchlight's beam,
>In falling stars…in planes aflame,
>As flak bursts flash out in the night.
Against my wish, against my will,
After all these years I see it still,
Time has eased the anguished pain
And memory takes me back again
On each and every day,
Glad to be alive,
To face more nights,
More struggles to survive.
Long those days and nights are gone,
Except for memories alone,
That will stay with us until life's ends,
So here's a toast: "To absent friends"

Harry Brown D.F.M. (50 and 223 Squadrons)

31

Per Ardua Ad Astra

"Per Ardua ad Astra"
A flickering memory stays –
A grateful token given,
To those most memorable days.
To reach a goal together
Strive
Perhaps with luck
To stay alive.
Seven young lives – a team
But one.
To serve their country
Right or wrong.
To fight for freedom – and the weak,
Each country's flag unfurled,
To lift oppression
And to seek
Pure freedom for the world.

To fly by day,
And fly by night,
The destined target seek.
Opposition always strong,
Never, never weak.
Dark clouds of 'Flak'
Night-fighters too,
Tired eyes to search the gloom,
Accepted as the job you chose,
The one you want to do.
Proud to wear that uniform
To belong and to be seen
In the finest force of fighters
That this world has ever seen.

Geoffrey Ginn (218 Squadron.)

Never Go Back, They Say

I went back to the old field
At the close of an Autumn day.
To find the tower crumbling,
The hangars filled with hay.

The dead leaves swirled and eddied
And crunched beneath my feet.
This concrete base, complete with plough,
Was once the gunner's hut.

What could it be, what was it
That I had come to find?
Traces of my vanished youth,
Or was it piece of mind?
The shadows darkened, lengthened,
As I slowly strolled around,
Stood and looked and listened
As they crept along the ground.

And then I heard – or did I?
A faintly mocking laugh,
The tinkle of a spanner,
The chuckle of a WAAF.

The muted sound of Merlins,
Throttles eased by ghostly hands,
Screech of tyres on tarmac,
The lost coming into to land.

For here were ghosts in plenty,
Young ghosts of yesteryear,
But I am young no longer
And am not wanted here.

I went back to the old field
At the close of an Autumn day.
I wish to god I'd listened,
And I had stayed away.

Roy Collins (90 Squadron)

Thoughts of an Air Gunner

(Written after a 'Dicey do')

We do not fly on sun-kissed wings,
To flirt with fleecy clouds as birds that sing,
And prove the day's new promise that may bring
New beauty to this earth.
No. Dark our purpose and our craft,
With deadly load we cruise the night,
Our courage the only thing that's bright
In this our hate-filled, fate-filled flight.
That is but one step on freedom's path,
For those who value freedom's worth.

While others, trembling, wait to feel
The weight of the invader's heel,
Our brothers' gathering strength to fight anew;
We carry arms against the foe,
And strike alone to let him know
He can be hurt – though we are few,
We will deny him victory.
To no-one will we bend the knee –
If die we must – then we'll die free.

If we are lost upon this road,
Giving our young men's lives;
God-willing true to our fathers' code
We will face our foes
And – grimly – we will die a-killing.

Anonymous 1943

Those Boys of Tender Years

(A night raid saga)

The scene a wartime airfield,
The time, dark winters night.
A cast of fresh faced bomber crews
Who looked too young to fight;
Stood dwarfed by a huge black aircraft,
Each bomb-bay stored with death,
All making gentle banter,
But they spoke with bated breath;
For this was war, they knew the score,
And each had secret fears;
Would they survive and stay alive,
Those boys of tender years?

Briefing was long over,
The prelude to their flight,
Where Kiel had been presented
As their target for the night.
Some had written letters
To their loved ones, near and far,
To families and sweethearts
Who despised the cruel war;
Who cherished them and prayed for them,
Each prayer through silent tears;
"Let them survive, keep them alive"
Those boys of tender years.

Came the time for battle,
For Crews to climb aboard,
The dark night's silence shattered
As aircraft engines roared.
Preliminaries over,
All checked from rear to fore,
The aircraft taxied forward with
Young men bound for war.
And though so young, their songs unsung,
Their courage knew no peers;
Could they survive, remain alive?
Those boys of tender years.

Speeding down the runway
With throttles open wide,
Sped four engine bombers,
Youthful airmen locked inside.
Their only guide the flare-path,
Ahead black inky sky;
Whilst lined along the runway
Silent comrades waved 'Goodbye'
The roar of engines faded,
Soon all was 'status quo'
Except for those young bomber crews
En route to meet the foe.

Climbing high above the sea
O'er which the target lay,
With outstretched wings
They sallied forth,
Nocturnal birds of prey.
The steady drone of engines,
All the power which sped them on,
Gave comfort to the airmen
For they knew what was to come.
Soon, very soon, the sounds of war
Would burst upon their ears,
A soul-destroying ordeal for
Those boys of tender years.

Onward, ever onward,
Towards a fate unknown;
Rear-gunner in his turret
So unnervingly alone.
Outside, the inky blackness,
Within, an eerie glow,
The target drawing nearer,
Eighteen thousand feet below.
And as they flew, these boys in blue,
All aircrew volunteers,
Bereft of hate to compensate;
Those boys of tender years.

"Target time ten minutes Skip"
The navigator spoke,

Then – just if they've overheard,
Each ground defense awoke.
A multitude of searchlights
Sought out those planes on high,
Illuminated fingers pirouetting in the sky;
With incandescent balls of fire
Ascending every beam,
Attempting to annihilate,
The British bomber stream.

With shell bursts all around them,
Each bomb-door open wide,
No armour plate to guard them
And no cloud in which to hide.
They gently heaved from side to side
To alternate their flight,
Attempting to elude those
Searching monoliths of light,
Which prey on the unwary
To implant the kiss of death,
Whilst bursting shells attempted
To extract the crew's last breath.

The crump of shells exploding,
The smell of cordite too,
Did nothing to allay the
Apprehension of the crew.
Air-gunners in their turrets,
Bomb-aimer in the nose,
Searched black skies all around them
For marauding One-One-Ohs
Which streak out of the darkness
Like a flash to strike and then
To disappear into the night,
Select – then strike again.

Within that hell, the cordite smell
From bursting shells on high,
Lay pungent in the nostrils
Of those warriors of the sky
Whose hearts were racing madly
And whose apprehension grew,

As through that holocaust of war
Unerringly they flew;
Into the thick of battle
Sped those airborne charioteers,
A palace date should decorate
Those boys of tender years.

Quite suddenly fate joined the fight,
No reason how, or why,
It guided beams of light to one
Doomed aircraft flying high.
One moment safe in darkness,
The next, death's probing light,
As every searchlight in the sky
Lit up that luckless 'kite'
And every ground based gun it seemed,
Belched flaming smoke and steel,
But, for that crew, no second chance,
No human rights appeal.

Those incandescent balls of fire
Which climbed each shaft of light,
Meant every single member
Of that crew would die tonight.
For them, the fight was over,
Each precious life o'er too;
All dead, the seven members of
That British bomber crew.
The blinding flash which lit the sky
And ended all their fears,
Deemed no return to loved ones
For those boys of tender years.

Many times that winters night
Fate dealt its cruel blow;
So many lives were ended
In the air, and down below.
Relentlessly the aircrews
Pressed home their fierce attack,
No time to think of danger,
And none for turning back.
And many deeds of courage,

Which never came to light,
Were acted out by aircrews
On that cold dark winters night.

Flying straight and level now,
Maintaining height and course,
Destruction rained from every plane
Within that bomber force.
Incendiaries, high explosives
With high pitched whistling sound;
Disintegrating dockyard
Installations on the ground.
Ignited broken gas mains and
The spreading fires' red glow
Destroyed the weakened morale
Of the enemy below.

Squadron after squadron flew
Like arrows from a bow.
Each crew intent on wiping out
The dockyards down below.
For some, it was their first time,
The rest had been before;
But all were aging quickly
As they fought that cruel war;
Except for those, whose proud young souls
Ascended heavenly stairs
To face a higher judgement sped
Those boys of tender years.

Ceaselessly the aircraft bombed
The target on the ground;
Then losing height they veered away,
A course for home was found.
Although not out of danger,
Relief showed on every face,
And fervent prayers were offered
For a safe return to base,
Where all the finer points of war
Were left to those on high;
It was not for them to reason,
-Just theirs to do or die.

The target now behind them
The sounds of battle o'er;
They left the burning hell on earth,
The aftermath of war.
For them, no wild elation
No feelings of remorse;
They'd merely done their duty
As a British bomber force.
No quarter asked, or given,
No bitterness or hate,
With only God's redeeming hand
To implement their fate.

Descending through the darkness,
Ahead, land of their birth,
Impatient for the feel of
Mother Nature's rich brown earth,
Whereon those gallant aircrews
Would gain a brief respite,
Thankful that the hand of fate
Had spared their lives that night.
Aware that soon new targets would
Be set by those on high.
To test once more the courage
Of those warriors of the sky.

So when the final shot is fired;
When peace reigns once again.
When memories of the sons who died
Invoke sad mothers' pain.
Be proud and sing the praises
Of those flying heroes who
Responded to the call to arms –
And died in Air Force blue.
They've shed their earthly bondage,
Dispensed with mortal fears;
Remember them forever as –
Those boys of tender years.

John Williams, (90 and 44 Squadrons)

Spectres

"And do the locals stand at dusk
Outside the Horse and Hound
To hear the noisy bombers' roar,
And count them off the ground
And do they lie before the dawn,
In cottage, manse and hall
And wonder if that lad from Fyfe
Will answer morning call?"

"A few still linger on, my lad
With fading memory stored
But all is silent at the 'drome,
Where once the bombers roared
Mild-eyed sheep now crop the sward
And larks in frolic soar
And only spectres from the past,
Still hear the bombers' roar."

"And what of nights when ops are scrubbed
When to the town we sped
To Lynn and Lincoln, York and Louth
With Harry, Dick and Ted
To drink and roister with the lads
And sing some bawdy songs
And shoot a line of daring deeds,
Which did not win us gongs!"

"The towns still have their hostelries
Where you were wont to call
Your name – with Harry, Dick and Ted's
Still marks the lounge-bar wall
And now and then a stranger calls
From far distant shore
And sits and muses on the past
And hears the bombers' roar"
"But is there peace now in the shires
O'er which we spread our wings
And is there cricket on the green
Where there were fairy rings.
And do the church bells ring their peals
Across the wold and fen

And do they mark our passing
The noisy bomber men?"

"There is but yet a fitful peace
And swift wings guard our shores
Descendants of our mongrel breed
And worthy of our cause.
And ancient bells ring rolling peals
Across the wold and fen
And you are not forgotten
The noisy bomber men."

G.E. Cocker (218 Squadron)

Missing

Less said the better,
The bill unpaid, the dead letter,
No roses at the end
Of Smith my friend.

Last words don't matter,
And there are none to flatter,
Words will not fill the post
Of Smith the ghost.

For Smith, our brother,
Only son of loving mother,
The ocean lifted, stirred,
Leaving no word.

John Pudney

Requiem for a Rear Gunner

And should you weep for him, if so inclined,
Then mingle knowledge with your gift of tears,
Bare not your heart alone – unveil your mind
Upon the history of his nineteen years.

He kicked a ball in narrow London streets
Then pedalled groceries round Walthamstow;
He learnt of love in cheaper Gaumont seats,
Set it to jazz-time on his radio.

He had a wife for seven magic nights,
His eyes grew softer in a small hotel;
They shared a dream of London, rich with lights
And all the things that Woolworths has to sell.

He sat, the sergeant-child, among his crew
And heard with awe the gross Great Man expound
The cult of polish – extol the sacred few
Who'd glistened long and loyally – on the ground.

Against his shaggy head he brushed a sleeve,
Within the barber's shop considered 'pride',
Bought contraceptives in the hope of leave,
Then flew to Nuremberg that night, and died.

Walter Clapham (408 Squadron)

The following poem was inspired by the yearly memorial service conducted in Dronton, Holland by the Burgermeister, and local dignitaries at the Allied Airmen's Memorial – a Lancaster propeller – in front of the Town Hall. It was the children walking forward to lay flowers on the memorial that touched the author to pen the following poem.

We Do Not Weep

We do not weep – nor count the cost,
As one by one, our friends were lost.
Nor wept we when the war's great toll
Took all the best of our young men.
We did not weep as we saw them go
Down to the storm of the mighty foe,
We did not weep – not once – not then,
Nor in the years to come,
When on parade to do them honour,
Came Kings and Queens and Chiefs of State
In pomp and splendor to relate,
How their cause was just, and justified
By the freedom bought as they fought and died.

We did not weep, not one – until,
In a little Dutch town, in a silence still;
The children came to honour our dead
Quietly – from out of the crowd,
With just aa few flowers – their little heads bowed,
In a line they came to lay them down
By the Lancaster prop - in Dronten Town.
And then – and then – despite our will,
We felt our watching eyes o'erfill
With tears – and yet we smiled.
How great the power of an innocent child.

Harry Brown (50 and 223 Squadrons)

The Gunner's Song

Now I'm an Air Force gunner
I ride the mighty 'Lanc',
I'm stationed with a squadron
Not far from Witham's bank.
We've had a pretty dicey time
These last few months or so,
I've seen a lot of Air Crew men –
Fine lads – just come and go.
Why it was just three months ago
We'd gunners forty-three,
But of that band of flying men,
There's just only me.
Still. I'll just go on flying
And sing the gunner's song;
I guess my turn has got to come,
How long, O Lord, how long?

At night we fly to Hamburg,
To Berlin or the Ruhr:
Another trip, another 'Op'
Will I ever end this tour?
Another flare, another fight,
Another airman dies;
The pungent air's our battlefield,
Our blood has stained the skies.
And it was just three months ago
When I was young and green;
While now they call us veterans,
Though my age is just nineteen.
Still. I'll just go on flying
And sing the gunner's song;
I guess my turn has got to come,
How long, O Lord, how long?
There Was Tommy. Dick and Harry,
Big Lofty, Bill and Ben,
And Jock, who nearly made it,
But crashed in Dunston Fen.
And Digger, Dai and Ginger,
Young Paddy, Mac and Ted;
A few of them are prisoners
But most of them are dead.

And will I be the next one?
I know that should I die,
There'll be a hearty welcome in
"That crew-room in the sky".
Still. I'll just go on flying
And sing the gunner's song;
I guess my turn has got to come,
How long, O Lord, how long?

They say that for each 'Lanc' shot down,
There's just one man survives.
While other plan the battles
We pay the bill with lives.
And mothers, wives and orphans
Must face the lonely years,
Nor all your fine memorials
Will wash away their tears.
And will this land remember
The young lives that we gave?
Or will we only be recalled
By numbers on a grave?
Still. I'll just go on flying
And sing the gunner's song;
I guess my turn has got to come,
How long, O Lord, how long?

Victor Cavendish (88, 106 and 83 Squadrons)

Our Place in Britain's History

The longbow-men of Crecy
The knights of Agincourt,
The warriors of Wellington,
Of Nelson and of Moore,
Established firm in glory
Gained a great, undying name
In our island's stormy story,
And so hold immortal fame.

The mud-martyrs of Flanders,
Men who died on Menin's top;
The sun-burned souls of Mafeking,
The slain of Spion Kop,
The lost ones of the Light Brigade,
Staunch stalwarts of our land,
All honoured in our history,
But what of our Command?

Our aircrew surely won their spurs
In Europe's flak-torn skies?
No moans from 'experts' then, no slurs,
No criticizing cries,
Night by night, t'was Britain's fight
They waged for many years;
By voice and pen exalted then
We learned 'Blood, toil and tears'.

Then no sneers – just praise and cheers;
"Good show! Destroy the Hun…
Do what he's doing to Coventry…
To Portsmouth – Islington"!
Each deadly flight to keep the light
Of freedom burning red….
Increased the cost – the counted lost –
Nigh sixty thousand dead!
Wounded, blinded, captured crew
Curved up to swell the score;
We paid the ever-rising price
With twenty thousand more.
But still the bomber crews pressed on
Courage conquering fear –

And – As the longbow-men of old,
Each one a volunteer.

'Confine the Kruppsmen in his lair'
Our 'Damsmen' doused his fire!
Darkening the Nazi factories glare
We lit his funeral pyre.
"Just what we want" The nation cried
Throughout those years – and yet,
When the war was done and won,
It just seemed to forget.

"A medal for your bomber crews?
Ridiculous" They said.
High decoration for your Chief?
You must have lost your head –
We've given him an OBE"
They cried in rising rage.
"He's not a politician
Or an actor from the stage!"

Ah well, OUR service recognized
Our bravest of the nation's
Men, who often did not see
Their well-earned decorations.
Our crews' reward perhaps will come
When in Valhalla's vault,
They are greeted by those men of old –
"Come in – your story has been told…
Come sit - above the salt!

Wm. R Rainford (38 Squadron)

So We Watched the Springtime Pass

So we watched the springtime pass,
And Summer gild the meadows deep
In buttercups as calm-eyed cattle
Wandered knee deep in grass;
And we watched the hot days sleep
In lazy mists among the hills,
And listened nightly to the roar
Of bombers riding out the light
And life seemed boring
When we spent the night
Poring over the squeaking set,
To watch the morning come at last,
And know that all were safely home
When the long hours had passed

By a former WAAF Wireless Operator.

How this poem conjures up the polar opposites of peacefulness and the horrors of war – SCA.

Four of the Best

Engines turning, coughing, firing,
Unchained power rends the night.
Four propellers spinning faster,
Wings vibrating, poised for flight.

Engines racing, throttles open,
Tailplane rising, airborne now.
Fight to lift the heavy bomb-load,
"Come on! Climb! You sluggish cow!"

Engines throb in steady rhythm,
Target's over there to port,
Keep your eyes peeled for the fighters,
Hearts beat faster, nerves stretched taut.

Over target, flak is heavy,
Engines roaring – bomb-load gone.
Weave and turn to beat the searchlights
Get a course to head for home.

Flak has hit the starboard outer,
Engine races – shudders – dies.
Probing fingers of the searchlights
Hold the aircraft – blind the eyes.

Heading back across the Channel,
Starboard inner's running rough,
Fight to maintain height and urging
"Fly you .... Do your stuff!"

Engines shut down in dispersal,
Props turn slower...slower... stop.
In the silence – 'Bless those engines'
Safely through another Op'.

Joe Mclaughlin

Runnymede

Go see the walls of Runnymede
And the names thereon inscribed,
Twenty thousand names you'll see
Of airmen who have died
With unknown graves to mark the place
In which their bodies lie.

The war was long and the war was wide
And scattered to the four winds,
Their moulded bones now hide,
Beneath jungle trees in steaming heat,
And Burma's monsoon lash.
Neath the Zuider Zee in a cockpit seat,
While above the grey waves wash.
And some I know just disappeared
In one bright flash of light,
That wiped the sky of plane and crew
From the backdrop of the night.

Yes, sorrow lives at Runnymede,
Its granite walls to hold
So many dreams that were not dreamed,
So many loves untold;
But love is there for each mother's son
Whose name doth hold his place
On these cold stones,
And that love you will find
Bestows serenity and peace
That's restful and most kind
To those who mourn.

Go see their place at Runnymede,
I am sure you will leave behind
Some of your sorrow
And a little love,
To help ease others' minds.

Victor Cavendish (88, 106 and 83 Squadrons)

The Branch Dinner

Gathering for the dinner,
They arrive two's and three's,
Those who walk with careful step
Some, still, with agile ease.
As each old gunner seeks the bar
To order foaming beer;
I see some as I'd known them,
Back on the squadron – yesteryear.

In bounces Bert, with greying hair,
His moustache somewhat skimpy,
No longer black and bushy
As on the nights he rode his 'Wimpy',
His searching eyes intent to send
The Messerschmitts to Hades.
They also searched around intent
On finding lovely ladies.

Now look, there's Ted, with polished head,
So corpulent and round,
If he was in a turret now
They'd never leave the ground.
But, in his day, old Ted would sway
And swing his browning guns
From side to side with gunner's pride,
While beating off the huns.

Len's just come in – the same old grin,
Though his face is paled and lined.
But his eyes' bright glow and bantering flow
Reveal the same clear mind.
As when he sat inside a 'Lanc'
With those sparkling eyes,
And he shot down many a One-One-Oh,
From hostile enemy skies,
Can that be George there in the door,
With a stick and shaky knees?
The boy who did two tours of Ops'
And won two D.F.C's?
As sergeant gained a D.F.M.
By his expert gunners fire,

Then finished up in forty-four
Behind the Sagan wire?

Jack, Jerry, Jim, they all steam in
To stand up at the bar.
Can these old stagers be the crew
Who won the bomber's war?
In Stirling, Halibag and 'Lanc'
O'er Hamburg, Ruhr and Saar,
In Wellingtons and Blenheims?
Good gracious. Yes – they are!

Beware now – for here comes Big Buster,
He surely did beat us all,
On the very first day of the last great affray
He answered Air Ministry's call.
It's too bad that nobody met him,
No witness who e'er saw him fly;
But we'll love his glories, amazed at his stories,
Of dicing with death in the sky.

The gong now sounds and as they yarn,
Their thoughts aren't here, you know;
But back in those cramped turrets
Which they flew in, long ago.
And as they drink together
Toast and talk in brothers' fun,
Deep from their minds they hear again
The rattle of the gun.

Bill Rainford (38 Squadron)

Tail End Albert

Ah'll tell thee a tale of young Albert,
  What 'e did up aloft all alone,
In t'tail of a Halifax bomber,
  What went on a raid to Cologne.
T'ground crew 'ad spent all the morning
  In stuffin' up aircraft wi' bombs;
T'crew put on all their warm clothing
  (Young Albert 'ad two pair o' combs.)
A comical figure were Albert
  By time preparations were done;
'E'd 'is stick with its 'orses 'ead 'andle
  To poke out through t'hole in 'is gun.

'E 'ad 'elmet and goggles and gauntlets,
  Flyin' boots, fur lined suit and Mae West;
'Is pockets 'ed stuffed full of 'umbugs,
  'Ed a large parachute on 'is chest.
When 'e tried to get into 'is turret,
  'E were too wide to go through t' ole;
T' Engineer Officer 'ad to be summoned
  To lever 'im in with a pole.
T'Bomber took off rather sudden,
  Young Albert were sortin' 'is gear,
When turret floor came up and 'it 'im
  An 'ell of a clout on 'is ear.

When t'bomber were over t' target,
  Young Albert came to with a start,
For a sample from Krupp's works at Essen
  'Ad 'it 'im in tenderest part.
This were not altogether surprisin'
  For as soon as the bombin' begun
T' 'ole of t' German defences
  Was chuckin' up muck by t' ton.
At that moment up come a night-fighter,
  Albert's mouth became suddenly dry,
So 'e popped in a ruddy gret 'umbug,
Shut 'is eyes, took 'is aim and let fly.

Pilot shouted, "What's 'e doin' at back end?"
  When 'e 'erd gun go off like a blizzard,
54

In reply Albert did nowt but gurgle –
  'Umbug 'ad stuck in 'is gizzard.
'E kept kept firin' 'is gun at t' fighter,
  While 'e coughed and endeavoured to talk,
When all of a sudden t' umbug
  Shot out of 'is mouth like a cork.
Jerry Pilot were all unsuspecting'
  Of missile approachin' its goal
T' umbug then struck 'im on t' side of 'is noddle
  And 'is aircraft fell out of control.

"Oh, good show!" said 'is pilot to Albert,
  "There ain't no other gunner like thee,
And when we get back to our airfield,
  Ah'll give thee an egg for thy tea!"
But when they got back they discovered,
  That there were no hegg to be 'ad,
So they went to consult t' Group Captain
  As to 'ow to reward t' brave lad.
D.F.M. it were not thought sufficient,
  They were all in a bit of a jam,
'Til at last they decided to give 'im
  A lovely great plateful of Spam!

Harry Holmes, (218 Squadron)

Donated by Andrew North, whose father was a pilot with 170 Squadron out of Hemswell. Apparently, Mr. North. Snr, in later life, was still able to recite it in its entirety!

The Deserted Airfield

Once more I stand on these broad sweeping acres
Where once the stripling Lords of the Air held sway.
Now, peaceful blow the gentle evening breezes;
A distant church bell marks the passing day.

No more the mighty monsters of destruction
With loads of mass oblivion stand.
Now, time transmuted, ply the wheeling ploughshares,
And men of harvest tend the fertile land.

Where once the hawks of war with raucous callings
The peaceful fields of air were menacing,
The songs of earth and sky are softly sounding
And smaller, gentler creatures now take wing.

And here's the spot where once-pulsating crew-rooms,
Now crumble into dust beside the trees.
I seem to see the forms of old companions;
Their laughing voices echo in the breeze.

Now heaps of rubble show the lively mess-halls
Where laughed and sang the fair young men of yore;
Who lived and loved with such gay abandon;
Who lived with death and so loved life the more.

No more I see the watchful-eyed control tower,
Gone to the waving wind-sock; dead the lights.
Alone I walk the corridors of memory
And hear again the sound of other nights.

But over there still stands the spreading village
Whose fair young maidens once we held so dear,
Alas! Those tender lips and sweet caresses,
Are now but golden dreams of yesteryear.

Here, once, I walked with footstep firm and eager,
Here, once, I laughed and sang with vigour strong.
But nearly two score years have passed; and sadly,
Now come the days of my September song.

I stand with one last thought for fallen comrades,

Should we still grieve, or should we envy them?
They grow not old as we grow old who linger,
"Age shall not weary, nor the years condemn"

For now it seems the things we fought and died for
Are not yet in our grasp and man is blind.
Land still with land is locked in mortal combat;
Are we to see the end of all mankind?

Ah! Surely not! The coming men of reason
Will see the bayonets sheathed; the banners furled.
Pray God our sons and daughters end the killing;
Pray God we'll yet see peace o'er all the world.

And now I quit the scene of old emotions;
I leave this place where poignant memories dwell.
Why wait here? A new tomorrow's calling.
Goodbye! Old friends: Goodbye and fair thee well.

Victor Cavendish (88, 106 and 83 Squadrons)

Stand Those Three Towers?

Stand those three towers still a-pointing
In the dawn light, stark and clear?
Does the ghostly roar of the 'Lanc' still soar
O'er the fields of Lincolnshire?

Do the shades of ancient Briton,
Of Roman, Saxon, Dane;
Still stand and gaze with mute amaze
On the ghosts who throng the plain?

Ghosts of the flower of England;
Of empire and allied kin;
Are they still in sight in the darkening light
Each dusk as the night rolls in?

Ghost of Geordie, Scouse and Cockney,
Of Yellowbelly and Tyke;
Do they fly again over Martin Fen;
O'er Grimsby and Boston Dyke?

And of Paddy, Jock and Taffy;
Of Aussie, Canuck and Yank.
Are they flying still over Lindum Hill,
O'er the Wash and Humber Bank?

And the Freedom Men of Europe;
New Zealand and Afric' dark;
Do they still fly strong to the Merlin's song
And the sound of the Browning's bark?

Do those hosts of glad young warriors
Still soar and fly and toil
And fight and die in an alien sky;
Still rest in an alien soil?

Ah! Many the distant lonely cross
And many the shattered plane,
Whose last home sight on a bomber's night
Was a view of Lincoln Lane.

Does that lumbering bus still rumble
Those lanes from – Thorpe to – by?
Does it still stop hard by the old churchyard
Where more of our brothers lie?

Sons of all the waring nations;
The plain men and the brave.
All troubles past; they've found their last
Safe home in an English grave.

While we, who they left behind them;
We few, as our years grow old
Still fight and fly in their battle sky
In dreams when the night is cold.

Ah! Lincoln! Our shire of memories
From the dawn to the setting sun;
Your heath and fen will live again
With us till our journey's run.

Victor Cavendish (88, 106 and 83 Squadrons)

Standards of Remembrance

If they could rise
And see the land they loved,
And perished for, in fiery foreign skies,
O'er seas, o'er sands, o'er plains,
Then count what now remains;
Would they sink back content?
Or would their standards which to them so-seemed
Worth death,
To pay for Britain's future, golden-gleamed,
Appear now spent?

If they could rise,
And call on us to stand.
To gaze on us through sorry, saddened eyes.
Would they, in national standards see
Self-interest, greed and laxity,
Their virtues cast away?
"Our lives, invested, now are gone,
Our long-proud memories stay.
Who will uphold our standards now?
Who will sustain them pray?"

If they could rise
And ask us please to answer,
God helping, we would make our firm replies.
"Yes. There are those that strive
To keep your standards yet alive,
Yours too are precepts that we hold.
Rest tranquil in your sleep,
We'll be custodians to keep
Your shining dreams –
As you knew them of old."

Bill Rainford (38 Squadron)

The Lowly Air Gunners

Much has been said of the "Immortal Few"
And the feats they accomplished
'Gainst Luftwaffe crew.
Many tales have been told of Bomber Command –
The pilots, bomb-aimers and W'ops of that band.

Then wonder of wonders, from out of the blue,
Mention was made of some other aircrew
By the chief of them all – 'Bomber' Harris was his name,
And the lowly air-gunners at last came to fame.

Yes, the chaps, who for hours, often shivered with cold,
Just ordinary fellows – not heroic or bold –
Constantly searching the enemy skies,
Traversing their turrets, straining their eyes.

To find the night fighters – determined were they
That constant surveillance would keep them at bay.
So look back with pride lads – and let no man say
That the lowly air-gunners did not have their day.

K. Spriggs (462 Squadron)

Tour Expired

Into the village of Sutton I drove,
To my old favourite pub, called "The Brook"
And sat reminiscing of hours spent with friends
Who had logged their last op' in their book.
They would say their goodbyes in the morning,
Perhaps never to meet again,
But the bond that had bound them together,
Through this life would always remain.
The custom of feet on the ceiling
Performed with much gusto and pride,
As the pilot would pen his name to the marks,
As emotion the crew tried to hide.
For this was their last night together;
Come the dawn they would all go their ways,
With only their memories to cherish,
Of "The Crew" and "The Old Flying Days".
The door of The Brook I threw open;
The landlord was one and the same,
I looked at the ceiling and said; "It's been done"
And he jokingly called me a name.
"You're one of the lads who flew from the 'drome!"
I nodded my head with a smile.
"Welcome back" he said with some feeling,
"I haven't seen you for a while"
The barman poured me a lager
And said "I was up there like you"
So I gave him an old battle order
To show when more exiles come through.

Ken Moore (75 (NZ) Squadron)

75 (N.Z.) Squadron at Mepal

On the village green, in homage they stood,
A proud and happy people,
Long lost friends, who met once more,
In their beloved Mepal.

This was a tryst they had cherished,
Since in youth they were rent far apart,
Proud veterans once more cleaved together
Bonded in mind and in heart.

Long ago they had furrowed the heavens,
Through death's darkening vale they had flown,
The gaps in the ranks told the price that was paid,
In Valhalla ring the voices they'd known.

Bareheaded and filled with emotion,
The survivors offered their prayer,
While the clouds drifted by in a now silent sky
Where once Lancasters took to the air.

No Cathedral with all of its splendour
Was a holier place now to pray,
For they stood with a host of heavenly friends
Together – at Mepal – That day.

Ken Moore (75(NZ) Squadron)

Ode to the WOP/AG

It takes guts to be a WOP/AG
And sit out in the tail
When the Focke-Wulfs are coming in
And the slugs begin to hail.

The pilot's just a chauffeur
As he only flies the plane,
We do all the ******* fighting
And take all ******* Blame.

We have all the shooting
At these ******* Axis swine,
All the pilot ever shoots
Is his horrible ******* line.

The pilot and the observer
Each has his tons of room,
We're caged in a ******* turret
And it's like a ******* tomb.

When the ******* flak gets sticky,
And things are looking hot,
The pilot hopes his WOP/AG
Will save the ******* lot.

Then if the kite should ditch itself
Into the raging sea,
Who throws the ******* dinghy out?
The poor old WOP/AG.

And when we're on the ocean,
With a hundred miles to go,
The pilot yells at his WOP/AG
"Row! You ******* Row!".

Then when each trip is over
And the crew to the mess all fly,
You'll find the poor old WOP/AG
Still doing his D.I.

But when its cleaning Browning guns,
The Observer's always late,
He does not seem to realise
That he's the Gunner's Mate.

But when this war is over,
And they add the final score,
They'll find it was the WOP/AG
Who won this ******* war.

So hail then to the WOP/AG
For he's the best of man.
If he can't bring the aircraft back;
No other ******* can!

Dave Webster (38 Squadron)

*This made me laugh. This gentleman was obviously recalling his memories of the link between the Air Gunners and those back at his station. I'll leave you to fill out the *******s! – SCA.*

The Sad Tale of a Straight A.G.

Now this is a tale of a straight A.G.
Who later became a Gunner lll
But unfortunately not before
He did five years as a Gunner lV,
Throughout the war he fought with skill,
Full many a fighter did he kill;
For which he got eight campaign bars,
The D.F.M. – and sixteen bars.
He ended up a W.O.
And even called the Wingco 'Joe',
And everybody said that he
Was a simply first rate A.G.
One day to his dismay he read
That Gunnery as a trade was dead;
"Blimey" he said "I'd better go
And sort this out with my C.O."
They argued long, they argued loud,
But a good air gunner can't be cowed;
The C.O. on his desk did beat,
And yelled at last "You're obsolete!!!"
Our A.G. slowly lost his grin
And bopped the C.O on the chin;
Then seizing him by collar band,
Hung him on his own hat-stand.
The court took quite a lenient view
Of such a natural thing to do,
And as he had not sinned before,
They broke him down to Gunner lV;
The moral of this tale is plain –
From violence there's nought to gain;
So if you get in a frightful stew
Just use the 'Turret' to air your view.

"Seafirer"

Pro Bono Editoro

I like to get The Turret
And read the gen inside;
I like to see myself in print –
It fills me full of pride.

I show my friends and family
The bright things that I wrote,
Until they are so tired they'd like
To ram them down my throat.

I like to read the jottings
Of my colleagues who write, too,
But it doesn't take me very long
Because they are so few!

I've always thought I was select
But not to this extent;
That I am one of such a few
Who seem to have the bent.

For putting pen to paper
In prose, or verse or song,
I always thought A.G.'s could write,
But maybe I was wrong!

To support the editorial cry,
I feel I have the right,
And so I'm writing this to ask
If no-one else can write?

The 'Turret' is a wizard mag,
And if you like it too,
Pick up your pen, come on, be men,
And show what you can do!

"Seafirer"

2. Other Bomber Command Poems

Bomber Command

You knew them when the skies were grey,
Those carefree chaps with soul so gay.
You knew them in the local inn,
You took them home, you asked them in.
You've seen their crazy, happy games,
You knew them all, but not their names.
You've seen them rolling back at night,
'Another crazy airman - tight'.
But did you know the other fellow,
Cool - though scared, he wasn't yellow,
When he helped to fly a plane,
He prayed that he'd come back again.
Yes, scared he was but on he flew,
The night was cold and friendless too,
For out there in the inky black,
Were foemen waiting to attack.
He longed to see this horror through,
He yearned to see his loved ones too,
The home he loves waits his return,
'Pray God, tonight is not our turn.'
He sees the target up ahead,
A stick of greens, the fading red,
The time has come to keep the date,
'Press on you chaps, we can't be late.'
His brow is cold, and yet it's wet.
'It's too damn cold, it can't be sweat.'
He feels his pulses beating fast,
How much longer must this last?
A voice speaks - somewhere in the nose,
'Left, left, steady - there she goes.'
The aircraft lifts, the bombs away,
Another little debt to pay.
The flak is rather heavy now,
A little frown is on his brow.
A sudden jar, a burst of flame,
A shell - it must have had his name,
He strives like mad to gain control,

To get back home his only goal.
But all his struggles were in vain,
They saw saw his prang, they felt his pain.
They came back home the tale to tell,
How well he flew, how brave he fell.
Your eyes grow dim, you droop your head,
You can't believe that he is dead.
Your soul within you now is stirred,
Your mind recalls a poem you've heard,
He is not dead, he could not die,
So young he was and gay,
So gallant and so brave a soul could never pass away.

Ken W Marshall, DFC. (578 Squadron)

This poem was written by my father in 1944, and he later dedicated it to one of his friends, Sgt. Reg Castlehall, who went 'Missing in Action' on 5th December 1944. Dad served a full tour as the F/E on Geoff Saunders' crew at Burn on 578 Squadron, from April to the end of September, 1944 – KM.

Rear Gunner

I feared for him.
His mind.
What he saw
hurtling backwards
to his private war.

He could spare only
A fleeting thought
For the enemy, in the city,
Staring up, or hiding from the sound,
Of a thousand Merlins
Circling around.

When he glanced down
Into the target's molten lead
Incinerating the living,
Or dead!
Suspended four miles high,
In fear and cold,
It was retaliation
He'd been told.

What words descriptive enough to tell,
Of a comradeship in hell.
Or explain
What the torment was like
To have to come again, again.
Eight hours or more
Is an age – on age!
With only a perspcapsule
For a stage.

As his friends,
Torn asunder in the tortured air
To know only roundabout
The dank, grey clouds,
As shrouds!

On return to base
He couldn't grieve;
Or a quiet moment spend,

Or really quite believe
The absence of a particular friend.
From another crew
Who only yesterday he knew.
In any case, it wasn't done.
There is no 'ops' tonight
An evening out instead
Maybe only a twenty four hour future
lies ahead.
Drink too many beers!   Dance!
Find a girl! Laugh! Sing! -   anything.
To hide that inner mind
Already dead.

At times his face
Told of a recent leave
Normality to retrace.
Not this hideous make believe,
This stark, unreal contrast to home
Where there was 'sameness'
Nothing re-arranged.
In the sudden quietness of his room
Staring, dreadful at the papered wall
In his own bed curled
Sheltered briefly from that other world
Trying the everyday things to recall.

Down the Lane,
The old stone school.
Village tea shops, bright awnings
Steadfast chapel, Boys' Brigade,
And breakfast on slow Sunday mornings.

The war took its course
He older, but young in years
Still has no tears.
I feared for him more then
For what he saw, now lies
Deep, unanswered in his eyes.

Some evenings in the village inn
At times, he hears the idle talk begin
And at the outside of the crowd
He quietly leaves
And has to be alone.
Hardly speaking, yet not proud
Not feeling better than they
Because he had hardly anything to say.
As he walks, his mind still wanders,
And in so many different ways
Living in the memory
Of their living days.

Ron Smith DFM (626 and 156 PFF Squadrons). Courtesy of Stewart Smith, Ron Smith's son.

Not Forgotten Lady

We first met in 1944, when I was twenty years old.

She was much younger than I, but I took to her on first sight.

There was no reaction from her, but then I didn't expect there would be.

The relationship, as far as she was concerned, was of a working nature,

As long as I carried out my part of the bargain to the best of my ability I would hear no complaint from her.

Her function was to carry out the purpose for which she and I had been engaged

And in doing just that, we would get along fine together.

We didn't spend all our time in each other's company,

I often went out with my pals

Whilst she was occasionally taken out by someone else.

This arrangement in no way affected the close relationship which was forged between us.

I was with her on the eve of my twenty-first birthday and we didn't get back home 'til early next morning.

There were times when our partnership hit a rough patch and if it had not been for her tenacity, all my efforts might have been to no avail

The relationship lasted for just over four months, when I was obliged to move on

She passed into partnership with one of my colleagues after I left.

It is now over forty-seven years since we severed our relationship, but I shall never forget her as long as I live.

Farewell- LK809, 'H-How' Halifax Mk.III
'One of the very best!'

Ken W Marshall DFC, (578 Squadron) 1991.

Courtesy of Ken Marshall. Jr.

Ops On

I dreamed last night I was back again, with the chaps once again I stood;
There was Trev and Jimmy and Gordie - and Dick in serious mood
Geoff and Jack in a huddle, checking the course and the height,
Making a note of the weather, 'Buttoning the job up tight.'
The Winco giving his 'pep' talk, Intelligence giving the 'Gen',
The Met bloke with the usual bull, 'Good cover chaps - bout Ten-Ten',
But clearing up at the target, giving a spot-on view.'
'OK chaps' says the Wingco, 'Best of luck, now it's up to you.'
Out we stream to the crew truck, around the perimeter track,
Off at the kite and start checking, Where's that b-- trolley-acc?'
Give the old engines a warm up, check, them to see they're OK,
Ground crew busy around us, 'Right chaps -chocks away!'
Taxi her round to the runway, 'There goes the green, this is it.'
Roll her on for the take off, check her for maximum power,
Check skipper's safety belt fastened; take one last look at the tower.
Geoff puts the power on slowly, the 'old girl' responds with a will,
We swiftly climb into the darkness, 'a night hawk out for the kill'

Ken W Marshall DFC, (578 Squadron), 1949.

Courtesy of Ken Marshall. Jr.

In Memoriam

We've erected a statue to Harris, we've unveiled a statue of 'Butch'.
Our governments couldn't be bothered, for a man who gave Britain so much.
We've erected a statue of Harris, the men of Bomber Command
Batch's 'old Lags' have never forgotten the man for whom they'd still stand

But it's not just a statue of Harris, it's in memory of all those who died,
The fifty-five thousand five hundred who gave of their all for 'our side'.
It's a constant reminder of honour, standing up there in the Strand
Of the selfless devotion to duty by the men of Bomber Command.

We've erected our statue of Butch, a leader of stature so tall.
We've put up a memorial to Harris, who did what he did for us all
A symbol of all our endeavours, a memorial to all those who fell.
To a man who did what he had to, and he did it so bloody well.

The Germans and others objected, from somewhere they found the sheer gall,
To complain that we shouldn't remember the man who made Germany fall
They all got up and protested; with moans about Dresden, Cologne
And Berlin and quite a few others, forgetting the guilt that they own.

And what if that shiny black jackboot had been on the other foot?
They'd have erected their statues to Goering, and Goebbels and Hitler to boot.
But they wouldn't have confined them to Deutschland that we all could tell,
They'd have stuck them in occupied countries, we'd have had them in London
as well!

We could understand all the furore, if we'd put Harris up over there.
If we'd stuck him in Essen or Hamburg, somewhere we'd bombed from the air.
But we've erected this statue of Harris, we've put him outside Clement Danes.
We've put him up here in London, which was bombed by Luftwaffe planes.

We've erected our Memorial to Harris and to each and every 'Old Lag',
For the things we remember and others we can't, that at our memories nag.
Yes, we've unveiled our statue of Harris, it's up there so noble and new,
For the chaps whom we knew that didn't come back, it's for them and Bert
Harris too.

*Ken Marshall. Jr. Written shortly after the unveiling of the Bomber Command
Association's statue of Sir Arthur Harris, by H.M. Queen Elizabeth the Queen
Mother on Sunday, 31st May, 1992.*

Passing Over

Silver fish above the clouds
Rising, falling in the sun,
Floating through the endless sky
In an aura of silent wonder.

They change and change again,
Arranging up and down and back and forth,
A shoal of fish against the stream,
Inter-balancing in rise and fall.

Three miles below a microscopic breed,
As in a falling spell now sense an omnipresent throb
Stronger now-crescendo! Louder yet
Oh roar! roar! roar! the CLAMOUR!

Dying, dying, gone away
Linger on the greying day
The rumble of un-numberable guns.

But this above can hear no sound
The gentle ears have long shut out
The never ending crash, the savage rave
That like great trumpets on the Day of Judgement
Shakes the immaculate plain of heaven.

Among these palpable and thinking men
Encased within their fiery cans
The obliterating rant has overgrown infinity
And now becomes a silence.

Only to return again
In halfway hours of hungry sleep
And then the throbbing blast that now
They cannot hear will roar again,
Reincarnated in their sleepless dreams.

Colin Dudley. DFC, Navigator – Flt.Lt. Jim Allen's crew (578 Squadron).

Courtesy of Stephen Dudley, Colin's son. On leaving the RAF Colin Dudley went back to college and studied Art, became a lecturer, obtaining a doctorate. He authored several books on architecture. He retired to Australia to be near his daughter Celia. Colin was responsible for designing, making and donating the laurel wreath that adorns the front of the International Bomber Command Memorial, in Green Park, London. Colin was also my father's navigator on 578 squadron – SCA.

The following four poems are by **Louis Patrick Wooldridge D.F.C.** 51 and 578 Squadrons, RAF Snaith and Burn, Yorkshire. Bomber Command, 4 Group, 1943 and 1944, also Technical, Maintenance, Training, Fighter and Coastal Commands, 1939 to 1946. Louis was the Mid Upper Gunner on Flt.Lt. Jim Allen's crew. 578 squadron. (Courtesy of Mrs Frances Long, his daughter).

Knights of the Air

Amidst the night sky, studded with stars bright to fair,
Sometimes graced by a brilliant silvery moon, - at other times bare,
Borne upon outstretched wings of speed,
The R.A.F. 'Knights of the Air',
Upon their wood, fabric and metallic steeds,
Like their counterparts, the bold Knights of Old,
Rode out to give battle,
Not with shield and lance,
But to the accompaniment of cannon and machine gunfire rattle,
The fortunate few returning, albeit covered in surrounds of glory,
Whilst alas, the unfortunate many, by fate's decree, - their frames so bloody gory.

Thus all ye persons of the peacetime future who dare,
To visit the various wartime airfields, hangars, messes, and find them silent,
Derelict and in despair,
Listen intently, and give imaginative thought to that which one had been,
And it is possible, that once again the events of those years,
May yet again unfold and be seen,
Allowing perhaps to be heard, o'er the faint eerie sounds of cannon and machine-gunfire rattle,
The ghostly echoes of aero engines, mingling with the voices of the 'Knights of the Air'
As they once more fly the skies in spectral battle.

The Fighter Airman's Lament

(To the tune of: Home On The Range!)

Oh! Give me the sky,
With a fighter to fly,
And, the clouds, to around all day,
To dive down to earth in an heavenly mirth
And return towards the sun in rash play.

Oh! Give me the right
To take part in such flight
And if ever dawns the day
To my country, I must pay
Let it be, during the course of a fighter affray

The Coastal Airman's Lament

(To the tune of: Bury Me Down On The Lone Prairie)

O'er the deep green sea
During the day or night
We maintain our search
With unfailing sight
Seeking enemy craft
Of deep or shallow draft
Whether they may be
Upon, or beneath the sea.

And if by Chance
After being led a dance
Fate is to us so kind,
That we are fortunate to find
The enemy unseen
Whether surfaced, or submarine
It will become for us
The climax of our searching team!

The Bomber Airman's Lament

(To the tune of: Empty Saddles in the Old Corral)

Phantom bombers on the old airfields
Where do you fly tonight?
Are you off to visit Berlin, Hamburg, Nuremburg, or Mannheim?
Or somewhere in the Ruhr, east of the Rhine?

Phantom bombers on the old airfields
Where do you fly tonight?
Through a moonless or full moonlit sky
Giving battle as you fly
Returning shrouded, but with your spirits aces high!

Ghostly engines silenced by time
Outlined at dispersal by rings of rime
 With ghostly guns of noiseless rattle
Patiently waiting the phantom hours of battle

Phantom bombers on the old airfields
Where do you fly tonight?
If you will only wait for me to join you
In the air battles of long ago
It will be in the company of my old aircrew.

Missing 1944

Try not to worry - it will all work out right,
They said of the horror which happened last night.
The heart, they say, freezes as the words filter through,
An inner voice wonders "Are they talking to you?"

Yes, it's in your hands - or so it would seem
All your life's future, love, hope and dreams
Gone where? The words here don't say,
Just "Missing" but hopefully not for more than one day.

"For we do hear quite soon if they're put in the Cage,
Will keep you informed, we know you're engaged.
What else can we say that will help at this time
The Red Cross is helpful for throwing a line.

No other thoughts enter the mind when it's cold.
Only the memory remains when you're old
Of the joy until then and the years in between
Wondering always of what might have been.

As the not knowing how. Or not knowing the 'where'
It's all finished and just cold, utter despair
While they're to say, with eyes bright and bold,
"Well at least they are spared of not growing old."

So the heart adjusts and cuts those bits out -
Or so it is said - that's what life's all about.
Pick up the pieces and fit them all back
And get on with living - and keep dodging the flak.

Betty James.
In June 1944 Betty James was a WAAF at home on marriage leave, expecting her fiancé, Flt.Sgt. Douglas Burton, to join her that weekend. Douglas was a Mid Upper gunner on 76 Squadron flying in a Halifax B Mk III, LW644 (MP-O). Sadly, he and his whole crew were killed on a raid to bomb rail facilities at Amiens. The crew was Pilot - P/O. A. L. Johnston RCAF, Flight Engineer - Sgt. E. F. Lewis, Navigator - F.Sgt. H. Earl, Bomb Aimer - F.Sgt. G. F. Griffiths, Wireless Operator - Sgt. C. J. Trott, Douglas Burton was in the mid upper gun turret, and Sgt. A. Moult in the rear turret. All are now buried at Beauvais. Betty wrote this poem shortly after her bereavement. She is now in her 90s and lives in Diss.

Platonic Friendship –Frankie and Don

It happened at a place that lies on the East Coast
At a village called Lissett tha' knows
Where you take the mud cure and the air is so pure
That the icicles hang from your nose

Now at this 'ere place that lies on the East Coast
A lad met a lass – 'twas at night
She were corporal and he were a serg.
So self-discipline shone like a light

'Twas a friendship platonic so both of them said
No necking, no mushing, no pash
They talked of things worldly like poetry and art
And the mystery of dining hall hash.

This went on for some weeks,
this platonic friendship so pure
'Till a factor unknown entered the fray
And that's what completed the cure.

The moon was at full as they walked out the camp
And Frankie said Don 'What a sight'
Don said to Frankie 'to hell with the moon'
Let's hold hands, for once just tonight.

Well the rot had set in though you must blame the moon
Though Frankie helped the moon quite a lot
'Cos three weeks after this she said 'give us a kiss
Ain't friendship platonic just rot'

The moral of my tale may not seem so clear
But summed up it is something like this
That friendship platonic works up to a point
And the point is that first stolen kiss

By Ms. Crawford, Instigated by Joyce Wiggan (née Rochester). Courtesy of Margaret May, daughter of the Rev. Donald May DFC, 158 Sqn.

The Rev. Donald May (Don) DFC was a navigator, 158 squadron, based in Lissett, East Yorkshire. At the same time, he was applying to be a Methodist Minister. He was a member of the 158 Squadron Association until his death in

January 2009. Whilst at Lissett he met Frances May (Frankie), née Rochester, a WAAF, based close by at 158 Squadron HQ in Driffield. They were married for 58 years. This poem whilst not written by a crew member, it is about a crew member and a WAAF, written by a fellow WAAF, Ms. Crawford, instigated by my mother's twin sister who served alongside. The poem was read at the funeral of Frances May the wife of Rev. Donald May and the mother of Margaret May, their Daughter, who kindly forwarded this poem to us.

Heaven's Heroes

The Daylight fades and Circe's flaming Court
Now leaves the Heavens to Cynthia's care
'Neath which in darkness airy battles will be fought
Bloody and grim in the Enemy's Lair.

As darkness cloaks the world in solemn gloom
The vultures of the night take wing;
A host, a multitude of celestial doom
Death and ruin to the Foe to bring.

This ethereal Crusade, almost nightly made,
Grows in strength and numbers relentless;
Its purpose clear and great the fear
Of the Foe whose evil proceeds repentless.

Away o'er the sea they roar in the height
Their trumpet call is the engines' roar
Their battle cry fills the still fateful night
And brings terror as never before.

Their clarion call echoes thro air at large
Proclaiming and heralding their gallant charge
On and far o'er the sea the roaring stampede
Which no power of the enemy can ever impede.

As this host of winged death speeds on
The fury of the Foe thunders mighty and strong
Until at last they reach the fated town
And 'midst the awful scene their load goes down.

Fire and Shell
A flaming Hell
Searchlights gleaming,
Bomb loads screaming

Winged monsters roar in endless flow
Tons of death and destruction earthwards go
Here amidst this horrible fantasy
Unbelievable spectacle – Devil's prophesy

The fires of Hell lick the broken clouds
And smoke clouds now act as shrouds
For a city – once an enemy fort
Now in ruins – reduced to naught.

Diana, merciless hunter goddess she,
Is looking on and gloats with glee
This terrible holocaust to see

Plato too is a Devil now smiling
To see countless souls in his hands now piling
This gruesome orgy of death appalling

Mars has never before in all his life
Seen such bloody battle, merciless strife
But how aching is the heart of Hymen
Whose sole desire was love for all men

Bacchus too is sad in heart and tearful
When his men are in a war so fearful
For his Art is drink and all that's cheerful

When he and Pan and Morpheus too
Could bring such joy and love in lieu
If only these men would cease their cruelty
And follow their Arts with more assiduity.

The Earth trembles as the battle rages
Greater than those of bygone ages
Below – the roar of guns defending
The rain of bombs ever descending

The rumble and collapse of industrial might
Covering the sky with its funeral light.

And high above the incessant sound
Of engines and exploding round
Of bursting shells forming steel walls
And Aircraft engaged in grim duels.

The pains of the Reich are well stained with blood
Blood from the Heavens and from where a city stood
And the night's crusade has taken its price
In the choice of human sacrifice.

The battle is over but the city still burns
And is left behind as the flock homeward turns

Triumphant heroes of yet another fight
Against the evil enemy of peace and right
Even he with all his might
Could not stave off this judgement night.

True Valour these Sons of Achilles display
Holding high the Torch their fathers bore
And brandish it now with new and glorious ray
Thro' sky battlegrounds 'neath starry lore.

The charge of the Light Brigade
Was equalled by this night parade
Theirs too was a Valley of Death
Where oft man drew his last breath

Where many would fall to horrible fate
But yet they went on with renewed hate
Riding the Pegasus herd across Cynthia's way
To destroy the foe's might where 'ere it lay.

Soon the noise of battle may cease
And the world again may live in peace
With Victory won by these Air Invaders
Whose deeds will long survive the ages.

To our dear comrades who fell from up high
Thro' burning skies to foreign lands to die
The pen of Homer should immortalise
The deeds these Knights of the air exemplorise

They won their spurs through blood and toil
Of war above enemy soil
Time will not dim their glory
Eternal will be their story

Now they lie in graves unnamed
They fought and died, yet honour gained
Yet we shall meet again 'ere long
Beyond the Vales in Avalon

Where true Knights know the peace and joy of Paradise
And nights of terror are past and theirs the Heavenly Prize.

Heaven's Heroes was supplied by Paul Batman, written By Phil Batman. P/O with 156 PFF Squadron (Phil was Paul's great uncle). Phil Batman was shot down in January 1944 and became a POW. Phil wrote many stories and poems to pass the time while he was a POW at Stalag Luft 6 at Heydekrug in Lithuania which was the most northern of all the Stalags. He was on the Long March to freedom, and was a POW until the end of the war

Little Messers

Ten little Messerschmitt Me 109s
No one was weaving, then there were nine.
Nine little Messers, one took off late
Failed to find the rest, then there were eight.
Eight little Messers flying in heaven
Didn't see the smoke trails, then there were seven.
Seven plus little Messers flying in two vics
The plus was a Spitfire, then there were six.
Six little Messers descending in a dive
Forgot the sun behind them, then there were five
Five little Messers climbing up to war
Someone shouted "Schpitfeur", then there were four.
Four little Messers turning home for tea
Thought the flight was over, then there were three.
Three little Messers cruising through the blue
Admiring nature's beauty, then there were two.
Two little Messers thought it was a hun
Hadn't learnt the recognition, then there was one.
One little Messer playing T & R
Tried it once too often, and then there none!

This poem was donated by Geoff Wood, who found the poem, which was originally untitled, written his father's 1944 address book. Geoff does state although the poem is in his father's handwriting, he is not sure if his father was the actual author. However it is a good little poem, and worthy of inclusion. Geoff's father was Douglas (Woody) Wood, DFC, a pilot with 158 and 578 Squadrons.

A.G., RIP

They call him the Aerial Gunner,
His hopes they say are dim
And his life is said
To hang by a thread
That is long and weak and slim.

He loves his home and he loves his land.
For he gambles his life
In a cloud, found strife
In a game with the Reaper Grim.

His mount is a roaring dragon
That flashes across the sky
To take the dare
To the enemy fair
And to strike him down or die.

He is the knight of the upper air
And death his eternal foe,
Rides the tail
With his eerie wail
Wherever his steed may go.

You have to give him credit
For the job he does so well
For he brings her home
Though his steed may roam
To the very jaws of Hell.

He wears no rings and wears no gongs
For Sgt is his rank
But I've heard them tell
He fights like hell
And is proud of the title Joe.

There are others here in the upper air
And we cannot detract their fame,
For they make a crew, and the job they do
Regardless of death or fame.
But this is an ode to the Aerial Gunner
The hero who goes unsung
Though the enemy knows his deathly blows,
May mean his own death throws.

(All my own work – GCS.)

This poem was donated by Mellissa Shepherd. It was written by her father, George Charles Shepherd DFM, who was a Mid Upper Gunner with 115 squadron and then with 7 Squadron PFF (Pathfinders).

The Immortal Ten Thousand

Time was in the early nineteen forties
When half the world was once again at war,
Brave young men flew out on nightly sorties
To hostile lands beyond their native shore.

These were the men the new historian slanders
Who gave their lives to save the land we love,
Not down in the killing fields of Flanders
But in the black forbidding skies above.

Ten thousand was at most their frontline strength.
Like 'The Immortal Ten Thousand' of yore,
New men replaced the fallen 'till at length
A hundred thousand fell throughout the war.

As they droned their way through the starry night,
Searchlights, the sparkle of exploding shells
And the Night Fighter, that most dreaded sight,
Would oft-times alternate with quiet spells.

Then in a thrice the darkness was aflame,
A patch of glittering silver on the ground.
A badge of death and 'Target' was its name,
With skill and stealth in darkness it was found.

Soon that patch with yellow flames erupted,
As every plane let go its lethal load.
That was how each crew had been instructed,
And nothing their purpose would erode.

And those below, there's none for them would weep,
Or ever think about those ghastly scenes.
For those were the days when human life was cheap,
The end would always justify the means.

Then as they turned and set a course for base,
They saw around them little floating fires.
Deep in their hearts they knew in every case,
That what they saw were comrades' funeral pyres.

As ever in this war- torn world of strife,
The all too familiar tragic story.
They received in payment for a short life,
Their reward, eternal youth and glory.

This poem was written by Peter Gould and sent to the collators by his son, Christopher. Peter was a flight engineer with 61 and 97 Squadrons. He served twelve years in all in the RAF and retired as a Warrant Officer.

The Heart of the Dead

Here I stand alone, on the bed of death.
Falling, my brother's souls being taken.
Reaching out, their hands, their hands stone cold.
I kneel, hold their head in my sorrowful arms.
Finally, they lay, they lay to rest peacefully.

War. What is it for? Why do we go?
To take back our freedom.
To serve our country,
But lose our loved ones.

Fresh green grass swaying in the wind,
Once, but not now.
Bright blue skies, spread through the air,
Once, but not now.

War, not ended,
Today, tomorrow.
We are still fighting
For lives, boney fingers shaking.

So, if you see a poppy red,
Growing above the lifeless dead.
Just think what they have done for you.

Thank you.

The above is a special poem written by a ten year old girl, Charlie Newland-Shepherd. It was written as a result of a visit to Wragby Primary School, by Peter Jones and a Mr. Auton from the International Bomber Command Centre in Lincolnshire. The two men gave the children a talk on the role of Bomber Command in the war, and of the sacrifice made by so many crews who flew on operations. The poem was passed onto Ken Marshall by Mr. Peter Jones, with permission from Charlie's mother. Well done to Charlie Newland-Shepherd - SCA.

O Feelthy Fly

A fly flew into the grocery store,
He flew right in – by the front door,
He fluttered round the bacon,
And he fluttered round the ham,
And finally lit on the strawberry jam.

Oh feelthy fly, oh feelthy fly, oh feelthy fly, repulsive parasite.

The fly looked here, the fly looked there,
Under the table and under the chair,
And into the office which was nearly dark,
And there he spied the lady clerk.

Oh feelthy fly, oh feelthy fly, oh feelthy fly, repulsive parasite.

The fly lit on the lady's shoe,
Then up her stockings, both brand new.
And when it reached above the knee,
He sat down to see what he could see.

Oh feelthy fly, oh feelthy fly, oh feelthy fly, repulsive parasite.

The lady clerk when she felt that fly,
Settled upon her starboard thigh,
She spread her knees and held her breath,
And squashed that feelthy fly to death.

Oh feelthy fly, oh feelthy fly, oh feelthy fly, repulsive parasite.

Comment attached to this poem: 'To be sung in slow, solemn time with full bar room accompaniment. All the best of luck Wally. Philip Hyden.'

Courtesy of David Layne, son of Flt.Sgt. Wally Layne. W/Op (97 Sqn and POW)

Just Ahead

Streams of orange tracer, streams of red,
Are curving slowly upward, spark by spark,
Across the velvet curtain of dark,
Above them in a frantic galaxy,
The heavy barrage flickers ceaselessly.

And now the searchlights sweep from side to side,
We're weaving through them in a gentle glide.
They're getting closer now....They're on us! No!
They've swung away again! And to and fro,
The groping fingers claw the moonless night,
With dazzling beams of rigid, icy, light.

They have us, first a couple, then a third
Then dozens of them, like a giant bird.
The heavy bomber starts to soar and dip,
Writhing, within their cold remorseless grip,
Crr-ump! Crr-ump! They've got our range,
The heavy flak is bursting
Into puffs of sooty black,
That skim across the surface of our wings,
More violently the aircraft turns and swings,
But still the shells are bursting all around,
And still we hear that gritty, tearing sound.

A sudden swerve – the fiery cone runs past
It's lost us in the shrouding dark again,
It turns and fumbles for us, but in vain,
Left – left' Left – left again, a little right...
The target passes slowly though the sight
"Bombs gone" A dull vibration as they go,
Below us in the darkness far below,
A line of flashes darts across the town.

Our job is done, but even as we turn
The flak is moving up astern
The moment's lull is over.... once again,
And louder than the engines' vibrant roar,
We hear the sudden thump of it once more,
A few minutes pass.... We plunge about
And the barrage ends.... And we are out!

Beyond the tireless searchlights, bound for home
Along the cloud stream way that we have come.

Anon.

Courtesy of Corinne Mitchell. The poem was sent to Corinne Mitchell by Wing Commander John Ely Partridge., DSO., DFC & Bar. He was skipper of her father, John Henry Allen., DFM and crew with the Pathfinder Force, 83 Squadron. After 50 odd ops John Partridge went onto Don Bennett's Pathfinder staff while her father went to the PFF N.T.U.

The following two poems were written by Wing Commander Peter McDermott DFC, DFM. Of 61, 144, 608, and 162 Squadrons, and 16 OTU. They were donated by his son, Shaun McDermott (retired from the RAF himself!)

Hampden Bomber Operations – Winter 1941

I have ridden the night. Through towering clouds
I've pierced the dark, all terror gone away.
In the fascination of the task.
I've watched the stars – Polaris, faithful ever,
Somewhere on my port wing. And if Jack fails
To bring us back (t'would be because of wound
Or death – he's good) you'll have to do instead
And stick on my right shoulder all the way
'Til I hit Britain's coast. Then that's OK.
A lighthouse crawl, a QDM perhaps,
Or if that fails a Darky call will bring
The searchlights' fingers pointing to some field
Where we can land. It won't be base, but then
Who cares? The CO might – he wants us back
In time for next nights' briefing. Well, hard luck!

But I'm a jump ahead. I'm outward bound
Amidst the sombre majesty of night.
Watchful, but with the time to spare a glance
Around, enjoy the sights – the sounds are out,
Drowned by the engines' roar, unless the flak
Gets very close. Then if it's seen <u>and</u> heard
It's too damned close by far. What Ken would call
A half crown sixpence case. I asked him once
Just what that meant. His answer, somewhat crude,
Referred to his sphincter muscle's rate
Of sympathetic movement. He's a laugh!
A good chap though, keen eyed and handy with
His Vickers guns. And on the Geep he's just
About the best of all the wireless ops.

The sights. There's lots to see however dark
The night. Unless we're stuck in cloud. But then
St.Elmo's fire will dance it's merry jig
From prop tips; and kaleidoscopic scrawls
Sweep up the windscreen so you couldn't see
A London bus were it to find its way

In front of you. A London bus? I must
Be running short of oxygen. The gauge
Says still three quarters full. I tell you what –
Poetic images are dangerous. A London bus!
Where was I? Yes! I know,
Flying in a cloud. And there's another thing –
You watch the ice build up until it forms
Bloody great lumps on each projecting bit of metal.

The direction finding loop
(A useless bit of kit. The lines it gives
Should cross along your track, or nearly so.
But half the time they meet like parallels –
Not on the chart but infinity!
The Germans bend them, so they say. Which is
A damned unfriendly thing of them to do)
Grows twice its size. The mainplanes leading edge
Distorts with several inches of glazed ice.
You're buggered then! If you can't make one last
Despairing climb above the cloud, you'll drop –
Into clear air, you hope, and warm as well.
Not warm, nor clear? Then you've time ahead
Which is distinctly finite! But let's say
On this occasion all is well.

And so we have the sights. Strange lights below could be
A friendly Belgian, Dutchman, Frenchman, Dane
Flashing a greeting – his own way, perhaps,
To show defiance, telling us that there are friends around.
Damn! That's no friendly torch.
A master searchlight! Play it like a fish.
It comes towards you, wait as long as you dare
Then hard across it, hoping he'll be fooled
And overshoot. But this is no new boy
And we are held. Ye Gods! It feels like
Those nightmares dreamed which find you nude amongst
The crowds who've gathered in Trafalgar Square,
And no-one offers you a coat, a scarf,
Nothing to hide you from a thousand eyes.

Then on come other beams. We're coned. But sweat it out.
The cogs are whirring in the guns'

Computers. Give them time to set things up –
Then dive ahead, balls out, build up your speed.
The flak's behind – we hope – there's lots below;
Red, green, mauve, yellow, quite a show tonight.
Then, when the moment's right (we've not been hit –
It must be right) haul back the stick, a slight
Turn off. Maybe we'll lose them. Or they'll try
Some other chap. The sort who twists and turns
But stays within the apof the beams
Until the shell strikes home. You must lose height.
Not that we've much to spare. But give them some
And that will spoil their fun. Roughly ahead – The shortest way's the best.
And there's not more than twenty miles of searchlights in the belt.

It's over soon enough. On in the night.
Poor Jack, I've sugared up his plot. He'll add
A minute, two perhaps, to make the time
To target right, or thereabouts. We've got
From one to half past two (we've not yet learned
To concentrate in time). A call from Ken;
"There's some suspicious bastard out to port
And edging this way fast!. "Give him a burst".
Ken does. "No damage I can see, but he's
Taken the hint". Nine times from ten we find
That if it seems you're wakeful they'll sheer off
And look for someone else who's half asleep,
An easy victim. It's all one to them.
There's plenty in the sky without the risk
Of taking on a crew who will fire back.

We're individualists, we of the night.
Once airborne that is. On the ground we'll joke
And laugh and drink and talk with other crews;
Sorrow a bit when, not in frequently,
Some of the squadron aircraft don't return.
But in the air, It's us against the Hun,
And if another's shot down – well tough tit!
But once we've landed we are safe and so
We laugh and jest and live it up a bit,
Knowing it's odds on that will come the day
The chaps will, calm and studied, of us say
"They've bought it, then"; "Gone for a ball of chalk";

"Gone for a burton"; or "Gone for a shit".
All euphemistic efforts.

It would be a bloody nightmare if, each time there was
A "missing" chalked up on the ops room board
Against a crew, we all got too upset.
So, it's a joke almost, although doubtless there's
Some mother, wife or girlfriend who would love
To share it to allay her bitter grief.
I'm getting morbid. But my eyes still search
Unceasingly the sky from side to side
With just a glance across the panel's glow.
Comforting instruments. They'll soon betray
Incipient engine faults or failing power.
Or quickly show your flying's up the creek!
Mind you, they can play tricks when eyes are tired
Or if the oxygen supply runs low.

I've seen them redd'ning then, and that's a sign
Quickly to act, to check the tank contents
And get the hell down to a lower height.
"Are you there, Jack?" "Yes". "And you, Ken?"
"Cold as charity and that's damned chilly".
Part of a song. In unison we chant
"but not as cold as our poor Billy. He's
Dead, poor bastard, he's dead". A laugh, and then
"And you, tin gunner?" "Cold as Billy too,
And damned near dead. And I can't see a thing".
"Still, keep your eyes skinned. Given half a chance
Some Gerry bastard will slip in
And take a pot shot – you must get him first!"

The mike goes dead. Back in our lonely worlds,
Each with his tasks. Jack plotting all the time,
Ken taking broadcasts, logging everyone.
It's funny how upset they get at base
If, frozen, he does not return a log
Immaculate as Christ's conception. Well,
They've nothing else to do but warm their bums
And drink tea by the gallon while we fly,
And then moan if some coded mix of dots
And dashes is not entered in the log.

More searchlights and more flak. We ride them out
Although we hear the sharp metallic rap
As bits of shrapnel, rather tired by range,
Strike on the fuselage. We're getting near the target.

Comes Jack's voice: "The final leg.
Turn starboard onto one four oh and then
Ten minutes. The course out is one eight oh
For seven minutes, then head two six five
Magnetic" They are putting on a show
Ahead. Brock's Benefit describes it well.
Three cones of searchlights, solid with their hate.
At topmost level bursts of heavy flak,
Then trailing strings of green and yellow lights
Fill up the middle range, while lower down
A positively vicious mass of red
Means someone's catching it from twenty mill.

Dear God! We've got to go through that to drop
Our load. Be reasonable, you sods, and pick
on someone else, they will, not mine, O lord
Be done. "Bomb doors open". Now we're on
The last few seconds. "right a bit, hold steady".

PAC McDermott 9 Feb 1989 (courtesy of Shaun McDermott, his son.)

Requiscat 1943

Cry for him Pat. For Johnnie won't come home.
He's gone to higher glory as they say.
And if you want to think like that, feel free.
I saw him die, along with his whole crew;
And it was such a stupid split-arsed thing,
Flying too low over the North Sea waves
When there was every reason why he should
Have been at Angels One – a thousand feet –
To give sufficient cover as we flew
In line abreast. You see, we hoped to find
A dinghy in that area from last night.
It was a bit too near the other coast
For comfort – there was just a chance, we thought,
We'd have a scrap. But it was worth the risk
To find the dinghy. Well, if we'd done that
There would be glory of a kind – at least,
Great satisfaction – we'd planned to drop
Supplies of water, food and other things
To keep them happy while we called up base.
They'd send the Air/Sea Rescue chaps at once
In armed and high speed launches to the spot
To pick them up. But now it's all gone sour.
No dinghy found. No trace of Johnnie's plane –
A patch of foam, and that a transient sign,
To mark our Johnnie's grave, his five man crew
As well. He killed them, Pat, as sure as if
They had been soldiers on the other side.
Of course, their wives and mothers will not know.
I'll send a letter telling how they died
In action searching for their friends in need
Of succour. They can hate the Hun. Or fate
Or war in general. They should really hate
Your Johnnie, Pat. His crew had trusted him.
As, in after years, on village greens
Gathered round crosses they remember them,
They'll think they gave their lives for the great cause -
"A sweet and proper thing it is to die
For one's own country", as the poet wrote.
And what will you do Pat? Weep silently
For Johnnie's life? I'll tell you what I'll do.
I'll curse him for a stupid murderous oaf

Who killed five friends because he couldn't bare
Not to show off. Thank God he has no grave.
For on his tombstone should be clearly marked:
"Here lies a murderer". Their families mourn
Because five airmen put their trust in him.
He was not worthy of that trust. They died.
Cry for him, Pat, for Johnnie won't come home.
He's gone to higher glory as they say.

Peter McDermott, 23 March 1989 (courtesy of Shaun McDermott, his son).

What is Our Destination?

What is our destination?
Said Skipper with trepidation.
Hope it's not Berlin again,
Twice in a week is a bit of a pain.
Hope the flak isn't heavy,
And the fighters not too keen
I'm concentrating on where we are going,
Not worrying where we've been.

What is our destination today?
Ah, I see it's Berlin again.
I have a coach full of passengers,
All veterans but now in friendship's name.
This time they'll be glad to see us,
And we'll be welcome with open arms.
We'll be carrying our good wishes,
None of us bearing arms.

Amy and Holly of Bishop's Cleeve Primary School with W/O (Ret'd) Ken Staveley, Bomb Aimer, 514 Squadron.

I Will Remember

As I stand here today,
I look around at those who have come,
To Remember all of the spirits and souls
Lost to battle
Fighting for our freedom.
Each person has a memory,
A memory that contains love and triumph
A memory for a friend, or,
A memory for a loved one.
A memory that will last a lifetime.
As I look into the Veteran's faces,
I can see the pain.
The pain of seeing a friend,
Knowing he's right behind you,
And when you turn to him,
He's gone.
In his memory he sees his family,
His friends.
Wishing he wasn't there.
Not knowing if he will survive.
But as I look deeper into their faces,
I can find those memories,
Hidden in their eyes.
All of us weep,
Some not knowing the real pain, But those who do,
Weep with triumph and glory,
Knowing that all is Remembered,
On this Remembrance Day.
I will Remember.

Sarah Atchison, granddaughter of Sgt Ross Flemming RCAF, 514 Sqn Navigator.

Lou's Back

In ancient days a favourite phrase,
Was 'Lulu's back in town.'
But now the speech at Waterbeach,
'Lou Greenburgh's back in town.'
By wire and phone in bated tone
The news we circulate.
How lucky Lou from out the blue
Evaded Boche and fate.
'Tis said that Lou in kites he flew,
Ne'er used the exit door.
Holed by barrage in fuselage,
'What else are flak holes for?'
His narrow shave from watery grave,
'Neath Samson's watchful eye.
We thought that sure-completed tour
A cinch, the lucky guy.
When over France unlucky chance
Brought Lou and crew to ground.
With nil despair, Lou wandered there
Til homeward route was found.
Safe back at last, all danger past,
Lou sips a crafty gill,
To dissipate and cogitate,
He's had his share of 'mill'.
Now he can teach at Waterbeach
To all we other chaps,
What Lou can do, with lack of clue,
We too -can do -perhaps!

F/O Lou Greenburgh, DFC and Spam.
Missing – Maissy-Palaiseau 7/8 June 1944.
Arrived Waterbeach 20th August 1944.

Writer unknown, this note was on the 514 Sqn bulletin board, and was then found 53 years later. From 'Skid Row to Buckingham Palace', the autobiography of F/L Lou Greenburgh RCAF, DFC & Bar (Bomber Command Books 2016). 'Samson's watchful eye' refers to Lou having ditched his Lancaster MkII in the North Sea on his first op, to Berlin. The squadron CO, W/C Samson, assembled a scratch crew, flew out to Lou's last reported position 70 miles off the Norfolk coast, and found the entire crew alive but soggy.

3. POW Poetry

Flt. Sgt. Wally Layne, a Wireless Operator, with 97 Squadron, was shot down on 23/9/1943 in Lancaster JA708 on a raid to Mannheim. His son David Layne donated the following few poems, writing: "The poems I am sending you, under the heading 'POW Poetry' were all written by RAF types, I imagine Bomber Command but cannot guarantee. I think my Dad must have got into the Christmas brew, as he wrote this in his log book:-

"Starkle starkle little twink, who the hell you are you think?
I'm not under the alcofluence of incahol tho some thinkle peep I am.
I fool so feelish I don't know who is me
That the drunker I sit here the longer I get."

If

If you can save your brew when all around you
Have finished theirs and borrowed more
If you can run a racket when they doubt you
But make allowance for their racket too
If you can wait and not get tired of waiting
When someone makes a boob while on parade
Or stand out in the cold in your pyjamas
While Hauptmann Muller's weekly search is made
If you can hide when duty stooge is on you
If you can wash your shirt say twice a year
If you can keep your mind on harmless pastimes
And not dancing, women, wine and beer
If you can listen to another airman
Telling you his crown is on the way
And never breathe a word while he is moaning
While you have got at least three years back pay
If you can say "Wie Gehts" or else "Kartoffel"
Or ask a German if he has a light
Yours is the camp and all that's in it.
Here's your happy future clear and bright.

Wally Lane, with apologies to Kipling. Fallingbostel Oct. 11/44.

The Prisoners' Lament

Bloody times is bloody hard, bloody wire and bloody guard, bloody dogs in bloody yard.
Bloody, bloody, bloody

Bloody tea is bloody vile, bloody coffee makes you smile, bloody cocoa made in style.
Bloody, bloody, bloody

Bloody ice rinks, bloody mud, bloody skates no bloody good, sat where I once bloody stood.
Bloody, bloody, bloody

Bloody salmon's bloody queer, looks at you with bloody leer. Is it good? No bloody fear.
Bloody, bloody, bloody

Bloody bridge all bloody day, learning how to bloody play bloody Blackwell's bloody way.
 Bloody, bloody, bloody

Now and then, tho' bloody stale, censor hands out bloody mail, better draw the bloody veil.
Bloody, bloody, bloody

Bloody girlfriend drops me flat, like a dog on bloody mat, gets a Yank* like bloody that.
Bloody, bloody, bloody

Bloody sawdust in the bread, must have come from bloody bed, better all be bloody dead.
Bloody, bloody, bloody

Don't it get your bloody goat? Was it Shaw who bloody wrote? Where the hell's that bloody boat.
Bloody, bloody, bloody

Now I've reached the bloody end, nearly round the bloody bend, that's the general bloody trend.
Bloody, bloody, bloody.

Crosses

Each life has its crosses, and an airman gets his share,
From a trip across the ocean, to the envied "Croix de Guerre"

There are crosses by the censor, far too many it seems,
There are crosses in his letters, from the girlfriend of his dreams.

There's a cross that's worn by heroes, who have faced a hail of lead,
There's a cross when he is wounded, and one when he is dead.

But there is a little cross of mercy, that quite a few may own,
To a prisoner it is second, to that of God's alone.

It's a cross that's worn by women, when we see it we believe,
We recognise an angel, by the red cross on her sleeve.

"S.S. Kriegie"

She's tremendous, she's gigantic, Looking trim in every line
She's magnificent colossal, she's yet also mine
She's gloriously majestic, most refreshing to the eye
She's exciting in her nearness, for we know she's standing by

There'll be several Red Cross nurses lining up beside the quay
With a choice of drinks to choose from, NAAFI beer or NAAFI tea .
It's good bye to Red Cross parcels, no more vitaminised jam,
No more bully beef or salmon, no more appetising spam

No more personals for listing cigarettes or censored mail
When the ship called S.S. Kriegie speeds along the homeward trail
No more roll calls, no more searches, no more posterns seeking brew
No more blowers outside billets, no more air raids all day through

No more belt ups, no more 'arbeit' when your stomach's not so good
No more continental sauerkraut, no more scrounging bits of wood
No more visits down to sick bay, no more rackets, no more stew
No more reading propaganda like "The German point of view"

No more bedboards, no more combines, no more overcrowded space
No more cattle trucks to greet us as we move from place to place
No more barbed wire, no more searchlights, no more pine trees all around
No more compounds, no more circuits, when at last we're homeward bound.

The Saga of the Oldest Kriegie

Oh, were you out in the grim north east
Way up on the Baltic shore
Where the winter nights are six months long
And the days are even more
Where the bitter blast, a snow toothed fiend
Howls down the Russian steppes
Where socks get frozen to the feet
And the hands are covered in chappes
Where the great white silence covers all
And the only sound they say
Is the song of the Droski singing his love
In the mountains far away.
That's where the oldest Kriegie lives
A man both seer and hoary
Living on nutty and polar bear soup
The head of this story.
'Twas many years ago
Way back in 1940
That the oldest Kriegie in his plane
Embarked upon a sortie.
'Twas the sorta sortie a brave man shuns
And the coward runs away from
The kind our Hero hoped to Christ
He'd live to draw his pay from.
In the bright moonlight of a summer night
Our hero crossed the sea
He bombed the target and turned for home
But was jumped by a lone M.E.
And then there came a wary time
A time most wondrous tiring
They took him to a Kriegie camp
All ringed about with wiring
They counted oh they counted him
By day as well as night
Sideway, diagonally, backwards
But they couldn't get it right.
At last they hit upon a wheeze
That seemed both cute and neat
They fell the Kriegies in again

106

And counted all their feet.
And when the feet were counted
They divided them by two
But still the answer wasn't right
So they thought of something new
They went and got exited
And shouted with much zest
But it didn't do them any good
For the Kriegies weren't impressed.
Then they lined up all the Kriegies
At a time when most folk sleep
And made them file between two posts
So the Kriegies baaed like sheep.
And when the count was finished
And they added up the score
They found they'd far more Kriegies
Than they ever had before.
For in a well-run Kriegie camp
You may get lots of fun
But no fun quite as popular
As mucking up the Hun.

Anon.

Suspense

The prison camp so grim and bare
Within the hated wire
In barracks prisoners drawn and grey
Crouched huddle round a fire.
What will the German verdict be?
What will their minds conspire?
Outside the rain in torrents fall
Heavens ripped open wide
Hell! The suspense is terrible
If only we could hide
At last, long blasts, the silence breaks
Thank God! Roll calls inside!

Anon.

Epilogue

Wings!

For you the big drum thuds today;
For you the bugles blare.
The squadrons form – to honor you –
within the hollow square.
From all the months of striving for
You – this moment bright –
The sword touch to the shoulder;
Arise…. Sir Pilot Knight!

No alchemist but craftsmen we, who
Have a subtle feel
To draw the edge and temper of the
True and steadfast steel.
All pointed blades and stalwart, you
Will scribe a newer scroll –
A later list of daring when the tides
Of battle roll

The long horizons beckon where our
Frontier girds the world
So take you fair this guerdon ere
Your pennons are unfurled –
But gallant men may wear it, and
Meet to walk with kings –
Our accolade upon your breast. Your
Flying badge; Your WINGS!

Anon.

I found this poem stuck to one of the pages in the logbook of my father, Flt.Lt. J.H. Allen DFC. It was attached to a page from his 1942 diary. Sadly, this is the only page in existence from the diary. This was the day that my father gained his wings in the RAF, 28th May 1943.

Dad's diary entry for the 28th May 1943 read:

"14.14 hrs. Mountain Daylight Time. No.1 Ambition achieved. Received graph from Muriel.
Cabled June. Muriel Home. Party 2000 hrs."

My father had finished his training in Canada and was being transferred back to the UK for conversion onto bombers. June was to become my Mum and Muriel was a relative of whom I have no knowledge!

I include my own poem that I wrote and dedicated to my own father. He volunteered for the RAF in 1942 and trained as a bomber pilot, serving a full tour of 40 ops, with 578 Squadron from May '44 through to September '44, continuing in the RAF until 1947, and then only coming out on the insistence of his wife, June. However, he found that he could not get on in civilian life, and re-entered the RAF in 1951, continuing in service until 1975 where he was retired early on medical grounds. I feel now, that the poem should be dedicated to all those parents that served in Bomber Command – SCA.

Upon the Cloudless Sky

Fly upon the Cloudless Sky,
In amongst the stars so high!
Be at peace and suffer no pain,
And share new joy with Old Friends again!
And look down upon us,
As we in turn look up!
And each day as we think of you,
Hold our hand and guide us through,
To the time again, we all shall meet,
To hug, and kiss as we greet!
And then we shall all fly together,
Upon the Cloudless Sky, Forever!

Steve Allen – 29th August 2011.

These poems deserve to live on as a permanent memorial to the brave airmen and women of Bomber Command, whether they "Failed To Return" or served their time and came home from the war, carrying on with their interrupted lives and taking up where they left off. These people are now few and far between; and many of them have spoken little or not at all, of their contribution to the way of life that we all love and enjoy. We mostly only begin to find out about their early lives, when they have passed away and we go to sort through their belongings and correspondence that they leave behind for us, to read through and wonder.

To those veterans that are still with us, we salute you and offer our heartfelt gratitude to you, for your contribution in keeping us in the comfort, wealth and happiness that we enjoy today.

And finally, I feel that one particular poem, by Ron Smith DFM and from which this anthology borrows its title, makes a fitting end to the memories of those 57,861[1] brave men that flew in Bomber Command during WW2 who made the Ultimate Sacrifice and did not return from Operations – SCA.

---

[1] *The number of losses, as stated by the International Bomber Command Centre, Lincolnshire.*

These Are But Words

If this page,
you chance upon
now I am gone;
Remember me!
If you don't see me now,
and I keep that vow;
do not deride
the care I put aside
for you – unafraid!
Unknowing that the plans we made
were mine alone,
waiting by a silent telephone.

Do not fear for me,
or the barren enormity
without you!
Life goes on
Seasons come and go,
magic of Spring.
The first snow.
The restless seas
will still withhold
their ancient mysteries.

Remember only
the sun shone;
and these are but words,
you chance upon.

*I'd like to think that they are words of comfort for those loved ones left behind
to cope with their losses…..*

Steve Allen, 17th May 2020

Acknowledgements

J.H. Allen DFC, for the poem found taped to the log book page for 28th May 1943, the day he received his wings:

> *Wings!* (originally untitled, Author Anonymous)

Steve Allen:

> *Upon the Cloudless Sky*

Amy and Holly of Bishop's Cleeve Primary School with W/O (Ret'd) Ken Staveley, Bomb Aimer, 514 Squadron.

> *What is Our Destination?* (from 'Nothing Can Stop Us', Bomber Command Books, 2015.)

An anonymous former WAAF Wireless Operator.

> *So We Watched a Springtime Pass* (originally untitled)

An Unknown New Zealand Air Gunner.

> *Bird Life – The Lesser Brevet.*

Anonymous.

> *Absent Friends*
>
> *Lou's Back* (from 'Skid Row to Buckingham Palace', Bomber Command Books, 2016.)
>
> *To My Wellington Bomber* (contributed by WOP/AG. G.E.Radford (221 & 172 Squadrons))
>
> *Night Flight* – (Attributed to Noel Coward. Attempts to find the original copyright holder have been unsuccessful)
>
> *Thoughts of An Air Gunner*
>
> *Night Bombers*

Anonymous POWs: The following poems have been donated by David Layne as being possibly written by fellow POWs, as they appear in his father's collection of POW artefacts:

> *Crosses* (originally untitled)
>
> *"S.S. Kriegie"* – Anon.
>
> *The Saga of The Oldest Kriegie* - Anon.
>
> *Suspense* – Anon.
>
> *O Feelthy Fly* – believed to be by Philip Hyden

Sarah Atchison, granddaughter of Sgt Ross Flemming RCAF, 514 Sqn Navigator.
I Will Remember (from 'Striking Through Clouds', Bomber Command Books, 2014.)

Author anonymous, courtesy of Corinne Mitchell, daughter of John Henry Allen DFM, via Wing Commander John Ely Partridge DSO, DFC & Bar (both 83 PFF Squadron).
Just Ahead
'Bunny' Austin. 99, and 40 Squadrons
Lest We Forget

Phil Batman, Pilot Officer (156 PFF Squadron and POW), courtesy of his nephew, Paul Batman.
Heaven's Heroes

Harry Brown, DFM (50 and 223 Squadrons).
Memories
We Do Not Weep (originally Untitled - A poem in response to a memorial service in Holland)

Victor Cavendish (88, 106, and 83 Squadrons).
Airgunner's Day at Runnymede
A Tapping His Finger A WOP/AG Sat
Are You Alright Jack?
The Gunner's Song
Runnymede
The Deserted Airfield
Stand Those Three Towers?

Walter Clapham (408 Squadron)
Requiem For a Rear Gunner

George Cocker (218 Squadron).
Cologne 1942
Spectres

Roy Collins (90 Squadron).
Never Go Back – They Say

Ms. Crawford (WAAF), courtesy of Margaret May.
Platonic Friendship – Frankie And Don

113

Jim Davis (90 and 7 Squadron).
   Children of The Night. – (Bomber Command 1939-1945)

Colin J. Dudley DFC (578 Squadron), courtesy of his son Stephen Dudley.
   Passing Over

Geoffrey Ginn (218 Squadron).
   Per Ardua Ad Astra

Peter Gould, Flight Engineer, (61 and 97 Squadrons), courtesy of his son Christopher Gould.
   The Immortal Ten Thousand

Bill Hearn (90 Squadron).
   Odd Ode To Air-Gunners

Harry Holmes (218 Squadron).
   Tail End Albert (with apologies to "The Lion and Albert "by Marriott Edgar & Stanley Holloway)

Betty James (WAAF), via Ken Marshall Jnr.
   Missing 1944

F.J. Kelsh
   Operation Mild and Bitter

Wally Lane, Flt.Sgt., Wireless Operator, (97 Squadron and POW), courtesy of his son David Layne.
   Starkle, Starkle
   If (originally untitled, with apologies to Rudyard Kipling)
   The Prisoner's Lament

Ken Marshall Jr.
   In Memoriam

Ken W. Marshall DFC (578 Squadron), courtesy of his son, Ken Marshall Jr.
   Bomber Command
   Not Forgotten Lady
   Ops On.

Wing Commander Peter McDermott DFC. DFM, (61, 144, 608, and 162 Squadrons, and 16 OTU), courtesy of his son Shaun McDermott RAF (Ret'd).
Hampden Bomber Operations – Winter 1941
Requiscat 1943

Jack Mclaughlin.
Four of The Best

Squadron Leader 'Dusty' Miller (38, 69, 115, 148, & 458 Squadrons).
An Air-gunner's Lament

Ken Moore (75(NZ) Squadron).
Tour Expired
75 (NZ) Squadron at Mepal

Charlie Newland-Shepherd (aged 10) Wragby Primary School, with permission of her mother. Courtesy of Peter Jones, International Bomber Command Centre, Canwick Hill. Lincolnshire.
The Heart of The Dead.

Frank Newton (35, 206, and 84 Squadrons).
The Battle of Britain Memorial Flight

John Pudney
Air Gunner
Security
Missing

William R."Bill" Rainford (38 Squadron).
It Will Never Happen To Me.
Our Place in Britain's History
The Branch Dinner
Standards of Remembrance

"Seafirer"
The Sad Tale of a Straight A.G.
Pro Bono Editoro

George Charles Shepherd DFM, Mid Upper Gunner, (115 and 7 Squadrons), courtesy of his daughter Mellissa Shepherd.
A.G.RIP

Ron Smith DFM, Rear Gunner (626 and 156 PFF Squadrons), courtesy of his son Stewart Smith.
> *Rear Gunner*
> *These Are But Words.*

K. Spriggs (462 Squadron).
> *The Lowly Air Gunners*

Maria Steinweg-Ten-Horn – from Heelsum, Holland, contributed by Air Gunner K.Randall. 357 Squadron, SEAF
> *Sky Over Holland*

Dave Webster (38 Squadron).
> *Ode to The WOP/AG*

John Williams (90 and 44 Squadrons).
> *Those Boys of Tender Years*

Douglas "Woody" Wood. DFC (158 and 578 Squadrons), courtesy of his son, Geoff Wood.
> *Little Messers* (originally untitled)

Louis Patrick Wooldridge, DFC (51 and 578 Squadrons), courtesy of his daughter, Mrs. Frances Long.
> *Knights of The Air.*
> *The Fighter Airman's Lament*
> *The Coastal Airman's Lament*
> *The Bomber Airman's Lament*